D1410337

James Beard
Beard on Birds

James Beard

Beard on Birds

Newly Revised Edition

~

Illustrations by Karl Stuecklen

RUNNING PRESS
PHILADELPHIA · LONDON

9   8   7   6   5   4   3   2   1
Digit on the right indicates the number of this printing

Library of Congress Cataloging-in-Publication Number **00-132692**

ISBN 0-7624-0687-9

Editorial consultant: John Ferrone
Cover illustration: Dan Brown
Cover design: Toby Schmidt
Interior design: Bill Jones
Typography: Goudy

This book may be ordered by mail from the publisher.
Please include $2.50 for postage and handling.
But try your bookstore first!

Running Press Book Publishers
125 South Twenty-second Street
Philadelphia, Pennsylvania 19103-4399

Visit us on the web!
www.runningpress.com

Other books by James Beard

৵

Hors d'Oeuvre and Canapés

Cook It Outdoors

The Fireside Cookbook

Paris Cuisine
(with Alexander Watt)

James Beard's New Fish Cookery

How to Eat Better for Less Money
(with Sam Aaron)

The Complete Book of Outdoor Cookery
(with Helen Evans Brown)

The James Beard Cookbook

James Beard's Treasury of Outdoor Cooking

Delights and Prejudices

James Beard's Menus for Entertaining

*How to Eat (& Drink) Your Way Through
a French (or Italian) Menu*

James Beard's American Cookery

Beard on Bread

Beard on Food

James Beard's Theory & Practice of Good Cooking

The New James Beard

Beard on Pasta

James Beard's Simple Foods

Love and Kisses and a Halo of Truffles:
Letters to Helen Evans Brown

The Armchair James Beard

Contents

☙

Introductory Note

*I*t is wonderful for all of us who treasure James Beard to know that his works are being kept alive for everyone to enjoy. What a pleasure for those of us who knew Jim to read him again, and what a treasure and happy discovery for new generations who will now know him. He reads just as he talked, and to read him is like being with him, with all his warmth, humor, and wisdom.

Beard appeared on the American culinary scene in 1940, with his first book, *Hors d'Oeuvre and Canapés*, which is still in print more than fifty years later. Born in Portland, Oregon at the beginning of this century, he came from a food-loving background and started his own catering business after moving to New York in 1938. He soon began teaching, lecturing, giving culinary demonstrations, writing articles and more books (eventually twenty in all). Through the years he gradually became not only the leading culinary figure in the country, but "The Dean of American Cuisine." He remains with us as a treasured authority, and the James Beard Foundation, housed in his own home on West 12th Street in New York, keeps his image and his love of good food very much alive.

Beard was the quintessential American cook. Well-educated and well-traveled during his eighty-two years, he was familiar with many cuisines but he remained fundamentally American. He was a big man, over six feet tall, with a big belly, and huge hands. An endearing and always lively teacher, he loved people, loved his work, loved gossip, loved to eat, loved a good time.

I always remember him for his generosity toward others in the profession. For instance, when my French colleague, Simone Beck, came to New York for the publication of our first book, my husband and I knew no one at all in the food business, since we had been living abroad for fifteen years. Nobody had ever heard of us, but our book fortunately got a most complimentary review from Craig Claiborne in the *New York Times*. Although we had never met him before, it was Jim who greeted us warmly and introduced us to the New York food scene and its personalities. He wanted friends to meet friends, and he literally knew "everyone who was anyone" in the business. He was not only generous in bringing them together, but eager that they know each other. It was he who introduced us to the late Joe Baum of the then-famous Restaurant Associates and The Four Seasons, among other famous restaurants. He presented us to Jacques Pépin, at that time a young chef from France who was just making his way in New York, and to Elizabeth David, England's doyenne of food writers, as well as to many others.

It was not only that he knew everyone, he was also a living encyclopedia of culinary lore and history, and generous about sharing his knowledge. So often when I needed to know something about grains, for instance, I would call him and if the information was not right in his head, he would call back in a few minutes either with the answer or a source. This capability and memory served him well in his books and articles, as well as in conversation and in public interviews.

James A. Beard was an American treasure, and his books remain the American classics that deserve an honored place on the shelves of everyone who loves food.

—*Julia Child*
April 1, 1999

Foreword

༄

James Beard the author/teacher has been with me in the kitchen since 1975, when as a young culinary student immersed in classical French cuisine, I bought a copy of *Beard on Food*. Reading Beard was comforting to me, because despite his sophisticated palate and vast knowledge of food, he expresses sheer joy when writing about simple American foods, like hamburgers. As time passed, I bought more of his books. He became one of my favorite teachers.

The one and only time that I met James Beard was in 1983 at the *Cook's Magazine* ceremony in New York honoring the "Top 50 Who's Who of American Cooking" (which is now part of the James Beard Awards). I was honored to be among that group and especially to be in the company of Mr. Beard, whom I greatly admired. We spoke briefly. I wish I could have told him how his writings gave me (and possibly an entire generation of American chefs) the confidence to seek inspiration from our American roots, while respecting all that we learned from the Europeans.

James Beard was born in 1903, the same year as my beloved grandmother, Aida, who was born in Rome but lived most of her life in the United States. She was passionate about the ingredients she cooked with, and her food, both Italian and American, was simple and delicious. She admired James Beard, and I'm sure the feeling would have been mutual, had he ever tasted her food. My grandmother was part of what may possibly have been the last generation of great home cooks—and James Beard was their teacher. Mr. Beard's recipes speak to his generation; there is an assumed level of knowledge and skill. To one accustomed to cookbooks written in the last ten years, where every detail is explained in painstaking length, the recipes in *Beard on Birds* may seem brief. They are, but it's all there—all you need to know, if you practice culinary common sense.

It is worthwhile to really read James Beard, not just follow his recipes, because often the best stuff is tucked in between recipes, in head notes, chapter introductions, and recipes without precise measurements. He was very generous with his knowledge, and each of his books is packed full of wonderful ideas in addition to his recipes. In this volume, the chapter on chicken alone has more than enough information to be a book in itself by year 2000 standards.

Mr. Beard was much too prolific to be understood or defined by any one book; it is the vastness of his knowledge, revealed in his twenty books and countless other writings, that tells the whole story. *Beard on Birds* is a marvelous example of James Beard the teacher. Less chatty than some of his other works, where his voice is more of a writer/philosopher, this book is very thorough and gets right down to the nitty gritty with hundreds of good recipes and techniques for cooking poultry and game birds.

In the pages that follow, you will find great combinations like his famous Chicken with Forty Cloves of Garlic, Pheasant with Sauerkraut, and Quail with Scrapple. James Beard also offers us many international dishes, like Mexico's Chicken with Mole, Paella from Spain, and Djaj M'Kalli, a North African specialty. In *Beard on Birds*, he explores virtually every bird, including snipe, woodcock, wild turkey, partridge, quail, pheasant, and wild duck, and then gives you many options for each one! It is rare these days to find such a repertoire of game bird recipes—they are a very special part of this book.

Along with great soups, casseroles, pies, and little surprises like Pickled Lemons or Edna Lewis's Fried Chicken, you will encounter many of the great poultry classics like Chicken Kiev, Duck á l'Orange, Alsatian Style Goose, and Bread Sauce for Pheasant. Add to that every possible part of the bird and every technique known in the modern kitchen and there you have it—a book about birds as only the "Dean" could write it. *Beard on Birds* has the aura of a timepiece, and like most classics, I think it will continue to inspire those who take the time to study it.

—*Jasper White*
January 10, 2001

Editor's Note: Beard and Birds

೪

James Beard first aired his opinions about edible birds in the original version of this book, published in 1944 under the title *Fowl and Game Cookery*. In pairing fowl and game he was looking back to culinary tradition, but his introduction soon made it clear that he had ideas of his own. He cautioned cooks not to overdo chicken and turkey, to cool rather than refrigerate birds served cold, to think twice about the prescribed currant jelly with game, and to be honest about one's taste: "Don't pretend to like rare game if you really like it well done." All of which was advice that would hold up throughout his career.

In the same introduction Beard spoke nostalgically about the chicken jelly the family's Chinese cook used to make, a reminiscence repeated in his culinary memoir, *Delights and Prejudices*, and he recalled the quantities of feathered game that came to the family table: "Ducks by the score, pheasant aplenty, snipe, quail . . . and occasionally partridge and wild goose." He had a precocious palate and demanded his wild duck cooked for just fifteen minutes, while his mother had hers done for twenty. His father, on the other hand, liked his duck pot-roasted for two hours.

Beard did not mind his chicken a little pink at the joint either, a taste that some of his friends did not share. He was a "dark meat man," as he often said, and he felt that it was impossible to cook both white and dark meat to an equal state of perfection. If that meant the white meat came out of the oven or pan showing a gentle blush, that was fine with him. Next to dark meat, his preference of chicken parts were the gizzard and heart, but he had a lifelong aversion to chicken livers, though he obligingly included a few recipes for them in his book. All in all, chicken was one of his favorite foods, and it became a staple on his menu after he was forced to adopt a leaner diet. He sometimes cheated by feasting on Clay Triplette's Pan-Fried Chicken, declaring there was nothing better in the world than chicken beautifully fried or roasted.

Turkey was a poor relation of the chicken, as far as Beard was concerned, and it was totally blacklisted for a time after his 1942 Christmas trauma. He was doing basic training in the Air Corps in Miami that year, he reports in his memoir, and on Christmas Eve he and eleven other recruits carved four thousand pounds of turkey between midnight and dawn. He could not eat turkey for almost two years afterwards. When it was eventually reinstated, he wrote extensively and imaginatively on turkey cookery, and much of his advice is given here. His own holiday bird was invariably done with a simple tarragon-flavored bread-crumb stuffing, and rotated during roasting—with the aid of wads of paper towels—a technique that depends on the size of both the turkey and the cook.

Beard revised *Fowl and Game Cookery* in 1979, calling it this time, *Fowl and Game Bird Cookery*. He deleted directions for cooking squirrel, possum, raccoon, skunk, and other four-footed game but added a considerable number of recipes that had become part of his repertoire in the intervening years. He also noted the tremendous changes that had occurred in the poultry industry in three decades. In 1944, chicken was still a party dish, and if you wanted a really fresh one you had to go to a poultry farmer or a choice butcher. Even then you could not count on buying a bird already eviscerated. (The earlier book told you how to draw a chicken or turkey, if necessary.) Turkey was strictly for major occasions and was not the plump-breasted creature we take for granted nowadays. And there was no such convenience as chicken and turkey sold in parts. Though Beard lamented the lack of flavor in mass-produced poultry, he conceded there was compensation in being able to buy fresh birds in every supermarket across the country.

In the ten years since, the most significant change in the poultry industry has been the increased marketing of chicken and turkey parts, especially in boneless and skinless form. Less than 25 percent of chickens and less than 20 percent of turkeys produced in this country are now sold whole, according to the U.S.D.A. There is also a greater variety of birds to choose from. Fresh Cornish game hens, which were just being introduced in and around New York in the late seventies, are now widely available, and there are growing supplies of pheasant, quail, and squab. In some places you can find free-range chickens, the equivalent of the flavorful bird Beard remembered from his youth. If you look hard enough you can track down that rare creature, a fowl—a mature hen—incomparable for stewing and poaching. And in certain ethnic neighborhoods you will even see chickens hanging in the window with head, feet, and feathers intact, the way it all began.

This edition of Beard on the subject of birds adds twenty-five more of his recipes, ranging from classic chopped chicken livers to a lavish truffled turkey. What is true of all three editions of the book is that the birds of America have never been in better hands.

—*JOHN FERRONE*
1988

This newly revised edition of *Beard on Birds* bows to healthier, less lavish eating habits by slightly reducing the use of butter and cream in recipes throughout the book. Another half dozen Beard recipes have been added. The book that began life as *Fowl and Game Cookery* and metamorphosed into *Beard on Birds* is ready for a new generation of cooks.

J.F. 1999

Introduction

❧

When the original version of this book was first published in the 1940s, the marketing of poultry was considerably different than it is today. Chicken was still in the luxury class. One shopped around for the chubbiest birds, those that had the fullest breasts and were the most likely candidates for a good meal. Still, it was a chancy affair. Broilers were sometimes long, scrawny things that had very little meat, and roasters could be equally undernourished. However, one could get very good fowl (or "mature hens," as they were sometimes called), which made a wonderful *poule au pot* or excellent broth. And wonder of wonders, one also got hens that had lovely strings of eggs in them—unborn eggs, as it were—that were a delicacy for the sauce.

Nowadays, chickens have become almost uniform. They are raised in enormous plants, and some are not even allowed to touch ground during their short lifetime. Often they are given scientific feeding, whereas in earlier times they were allowed to roam at will and eat more or less what the family ate. They brought to the table flavors of good feeding and healthy developing. However, I think there are few of us who would exchange the present availability of chickens of all types for the doubtful shopping around that we used to do.

A friend and student of mine is the head of a chicken-producing plant in California that processes close to 400,000 chickens a day. These chickens are not raised on wire but are allowed to do some running. They are scientifically fed; consultants are on duty at all times to be certain that their food is balanced to promote growth, tenderness, and reproduction. There is practically no waste in these chickens: the feet are cleaned, frozen, and shipped to China, as the Chinese use chicken feet a great deal in their cuisine; and even the feathers are processed into a powder.

I have also toured chicken compounds in Oregon, where I get extremely good chickens that are fresh, flavorful, and extraordinarily clean. Cleanliness is one of the rules of the chicken industry—a situation that is markedly different from former days. I can remember the ordeal one faced before presenting a chicken at table: drawing it (being careful not to rupture the gall sack), washing off the waste materials that may have collected on the carcass, and singeing off the little hairs and pin feathers. I don't think any modern, up-to-date cook, or at least very few, knows how to draw a chicken any longer. All this is performed for us; and the neck and giblets are removed, washed, and put into a separate package, tucked into the cavity of the chicken. It is significant to note, too, that nowadays chickens are bred and cared for so well that they require less time to cook. Some people argue that there is no flavor left in a scientifically bred chicken, but I think that one finds a great variation in quality, from fair to excellent.

One interesting development in the marketing of chicken is the fact that we now have not only the whole birds, but individual parts. One can find legs and thighs, breasts, backs and necks, gizzards and hearts—all sold separately, which is a great convenience. Since I am a dark-meat man, I am far more apt to buy legs and thighs for a dish than I am to buy a whole chicken and cut it up. Likewise, the incredible number of people who specialize in serving chicken breast variations have a field day, for they can get them in abundance, either with bone or boned. In fancier markets the breast meat even comes filleted, much like veal. (One must remember that a chicken breast per se consists of two half breasts joined together by the breast bone. So if you are reading a recipe that calls for 8 chicken breasts, it is likely to mean 4 chicken breasts cut in half).

Another advantage of chicken parts is that one can use the backs, necks, and gizzards for stock and broth. The gizzards add such a gelatinous quality, as do the bones and necks. It is a very simple and wise practice to keep stock in the freezer at all times, and to use the gizzards for other dishes as well.

The only chicken product that is difficult to find these days— probably due to the way chickens are raised—is a hen or fowl, for poaching. I was mistakenly led to something called a "roasting fowl" one day that proved to be impregnable to cooking. It didn't even make good broth. Otherwise, one can generally trust the classifications that are given for chickens of all shapes, sizes, and qualities.

The raising and marketing of turkey has changed greatly in recent times also. For the most part, we now have turkeys that are much more compact, that are raised for a full, plump breast, a problem for those of us who love the dark meat. This used to be in short supply to begin with and is even more so now.

As with chickens, turkey in parts has become a most advantageous and intelligent way to buy turkeys when one is not going to have a large, roasted bird to grace the table. And speaking of that, it is apparent by now that turkey has evolved from being the sainted holiday bird for Thanksgiving, Christmas, and New Year's to an economical family dish used the year round and in many different ways. A turkey breast can be used for a hot meal and then for various cold dishes such as turkey tonnato or turkey salad. It can also be cut into scallops and used as one would use veal scallops. One breast will carry a family through several meals. The legs and thighs can be roasted, braised, and poached; or boned, stuffed, rolled, and cooked as a type of galantine or ballotine. Turkey wings, braised, sautéed, or curried, are delicious, especially for those who like to pick bones.

Turkeys are now available frozen with extra fat inserted into their breasts to create what is called "self-basting"; some have been injected with butter, others with vegetable oil. This presumably makes them more tender and flavorful. Fresh-killed birds are obtainable in most good butcher shops, and the sizes vary tremendously. Time was when only larger birds, from 12 to 20 pounds, were sold. Now it is possible to find smaller birds of 5 or 6 pounds to 9 pounds.

There are still wild turkeys to be hunted, too, and domestic wild turkeys can be found on some farms. If you are curious, you might buy one someday and compare its bone structure with that of the full-breasted birds that we have now. It is rather surprising to see what the ancestor of our holiday turkey looks like. As for flavor, I find it a far more delicious fowl.

Ducks are found in most parts of this country, and a large portion are sold frozen, cleaned, and processed as Long Island ducklings. They have an extremely heavy layer of fat on them and have to be cooked accordingly. One can occasionally find fresh-killed, meatier ducks. And in Pennsylvania, Muscovy duck, a much leaner bird than the Long Island, is commonplace in country markets during certain seasons. In San Francisco's Chinatown, and possibly in other Chinese communities, ducks are specially processed for what is called the "Buddhist trade." They are sold complete with head and feet and are perhaps the most perfectly cleaned birds I have ever seen. (They come from farms in Petaluma, which is not far from San Francisco.) If you live in a city with a large Chinese population, you will be well repaid for making a trip to one of their markets.

The raising and distribution of smaller birds has in general kept up with the industry with the exception of squabs, which are available in fewer places than they used to be. When I was young I remember squabs in many city markets—especially in San Francisco and New York—extremely reasonable and always available. On the other hand, a bird called the "Rock Cornish game hen or "game bird" has inundated our markets. For the most part, these small birds—a cross between a game cock and a Plymouth Rock hen—are sold processed and frozen, in which form I cannot recommend them. However, in the greater New York metropolitan area, one can buy fresh Cornish game hens that are remarkably delicious. They lend themselves admirably to most ways of preparing chicken; they brown nicely, are excellent stuffed and roasted at high temperature, and are extremely good sautéed very quickly.

There has been so much change and development in the poultry industry that it might well be the most efficient of all the food suppliers in the country from the standpoint of availability, quality control, and general excellence. In addition there are game farms in operation that produce fine quail, partridge, and pheasants—both baby pheasants and fully grown ones, which are sold fresh or frozen. The pheasants are produced primarily for the restaurant trade, which uses vast numbers of them for dinners and for catering. However, they are also available to the general public and provide a festive change from the usual poultry menu. Buy them fresh, if you can, and allow them to hang in a cool place or to mature in the refrigerator for a few days before you use them. They will have a much better flavor.

While the outlook for poultry and domesticated game birds has greatly improved, some birds from the wild are less plentiful than they once were; and for most Americans, grouse is no longer to be had at all. When the earlier version of this book was written, grouse was still being flown over in season from Europe for specialty food shops and certain restaurants. Government regulations now prohibit this. So unless you have a private source, you will have to migrate to England for part of the year, if you fancy this champion of all game birds.

—JAMES BEARD
1979

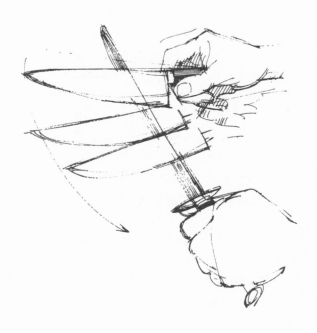

CHAPTER 1

Chicken

❧

Chicken Classifications

SQUAB CHICKEN
The youngest of chickens on the market, weighing about a pound, and usually broiled, either split or whole. You will need one per serving. Expensive and hard to find.

CORNISH GAME HEN
Young hens, weighing 1 to 1¾ pounds. You will need one per serving of the smaller birds. Use for roasting, sautéing, or broiling.

BROILERS
These are young birds, weighing 1½ to 2½ pounds, and extremely tender. They should be firmly meated, with a little fat on them. Use for broiling and some sautéing. Sometimes cooked whole, they are generally split in half. In this case, remove the back and neck with poultry shears and press down firmly to flatten the two halves and allow more even cooking. One half-broiler is considered a portion.

FRYERS OR BROILER-FRYERS

These all-purpose birds weigh between 2 and 3½ pounds. They are cooked either split, as is the case with broilers, or cut into smaller serving portions and broiled, sautéed, fried, or braised. Be sure to cut—do not chop—the chicken. Slice between the legs and body through the thigh joint. Cut each leg and thigh in half at the joint. Then cut through the wing joints. Next split the carcass, using poultry shears. The breast can be boned out or left intact and cut into two pieces; or, in the case of a large and meaty chicken, cut into three pieces. Cut the back and rib cage into two or three pieces. (Always include these for people who love to pick bones. I am one.) Thus, you can get as many as twelve pieces from one bird.

ROASTERS

Larger birds ranging from 4 to 6 pounds. They may be used for poaching as well as roasting.

CAPONS

Capons are unsexed male birds whose flesh is tender and delicate. These weigh up to 8 or 9 pounds and should be considered if you are serving more than four people. They are no longer hormone fed, due to government regulations, so you should feel quite safe in using them. More expensive than other chickens.

FOWL

A mature or old hen, used for poaching or for fricassees, and wonderful eating if you can find one. Ranging in weight from 4 to 8 pounds, they are usually well-retired layers. However, they are seldom found in markets nowadays, and the fowl that does appear is, in my opinion, only worthy of being used to make strong broth. Beware of something called a "roasting fowl"; it will never tenderize by roasting.

Sautéed Chicken

Chicken is sautéed as often as it is fried, although people tend to confuse the two terms. The difference lies in the amount of fat used. A small amount is used for sautéing; in frying, the food is well steeped in fat or entirely covered with it.

Buy broilers or small fryers for a sauté. Tiny chickens can be sautéed whole. Larger chickens should be cut in half or in convenient serving pieces. And be sure the giblets are included, for they make a sauté even better.

The prime utensil to use for this form of cookery is an iron skillet or sauté pan, although any heavy pan—cast aluminum, stainless steel, or enamel on iron—can be used. The pan should be equipped with a lid that fits tightly.

Any choice of fats can be used. Clarified butter is the finest, followed by olive oil, peanut oil, and corn oil; margarine gives acceptable results, too; and bacon fat is wonderful, although it brings another flavor into your dish.

To sauté, heat a light film of butter or other fat in the pan. Depending on the amount of chicken being prepared, you will generally need 2 to 5 tablespoons. Brown the chicken on all sides over a brisk flame, then cover and let tenderize over low heat. If you are making a sauce for the dish, remove the pieces of chicken to a hot platter while you prepare it. To rewarm, either return the chicken to the pan and heat with the sauce for a few moments, or keep the chicken warm on a hot platter and pour the sauce over it.

BASIC CHICKEN SAUTÉ

2 broilers or fryers, 2 pounds each
6 tablespoons butter
Flour for dredging (optional)
Salt and freshly ground black pepper
½ cup dry white wine
3 to 4 tablespoons chopped parsley

❧ Each chicken should be cut into four pieces—two breast halves with the wings attached, and the two legs and thighs with part of the backbone. Wipe the chicken with a damp cloth if you wish.

Sautés should not be overcrowded in the pan. Therefore, since you are preparing two chickens, it might be wise to use two pans, putting the white meat in one and the dark meat in the other, since they require different cooking times.

Melt the butter in one very large heavy skillet or two smaller ones with a tight-fitting lid or lids. Add the chicken pieces and brown them over medium-high heat on all sides. (For a deeper color, flour the chicken first.) Season to taste with salt and pepper, then reduce the heat, cover, and cook very gently for about 5 to 10 minutes. Remove the cover or covers and rearrange the pieces so they will cook evenly. Add ¼ cup wine, recover, and cook 10 minutes more. Uncover and move the pieces of white meat to the top (if using one skillet), leaving the dark meat, which takes longer to cook, on the bottom. Cover and cook until the chicken is just tender and done, but still juicy, about 5 to 10 minutes more.

Remove the chicken pieces to a hot platter. Add the remaining wine and the parsley to the pan or pans, turn up the heat, and boil, scraping up the brown glaze from the bottom with a wooden spoon. When the juices have reduced a little, pour over the chicken.

Serves four.

A SAUTÉ WITH WHITE WINE AND HERBS

2 broilers or fryers, 2 pounds each, quartered
6 tablespoons butter or butter and oil
1 medium onion, finely chopped
Salt and freshly ground black pepper
1 tablespoon each chopped fresh parsley, chives, chervil, and tarragon
  (or substitute 1 teaspoon dried herbs where necessary)
½ cup dry white wine
Lemon juice to taste

Brown the chicken pieces in the butter in one very large skillet or two smaller ones. Add the finely chopped onion, reduce the heat, and cover. Cook for about 10 minutes. Rearrange the pieces to cook evenly, and cook until tender, about 10 minutes more. Season to taste with salt and pepper, and add the herbs. Pour the wine over the chicken, cover, and let it cook down with the herbs, onion, and chicken juices. Degrease the sauce and correct the seasoning. Just before serving, add a few drops of freshly squeezed lemon juice. This is delicious with crusty fried potatoes and puréed spinach.

Serves four.

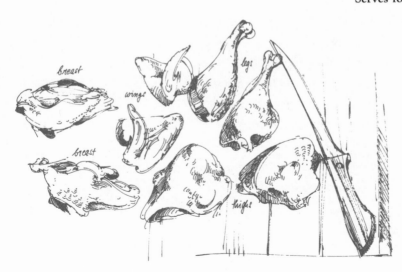

JEANNE OWEN'S SAUTÉ WITH TARRAGON

2 broilers, 2 pounds each, quartered
1 tablespoon dried or 2 tablespoons fresh tarragon
½ cup Riesling wine
6 tablespoons butter
Salt and freshly ground black pepper

❧ Prepare the broilers for sauté. If using dried tarragon soak in ¼ cup Riesling for 30 minutes. Melt the butter in one very large heavy skillet or two smaller ones and brown the pieces of chicken quickly. Add the remaining Riesling and reduce the heat. Add salt and pepper to taste. Cover and cook for 15 minutes. About 5 minutes before the chicken is done, add the fresh or soaked tarragon. Turn the chicken in this several times, then cook 5 to 10 minutes more, or until tender. Arrange on a hot platter. Swirl the pan juices over high heat for 2 minutes and pour over the chicken.

Serves four.

A SAUTÉ WITH TOMATO

2 broilers or fryers, 2 pounds each, quartered
6 tablespoons butter
Flour for dredging (optional)
Salt and freshly ground black pepper
3 tablespoons finely chopped onion
1 small clove garlic, finely chopped
½ cup dry white wine
3 medium tomatoes, peeled, seeded, and chopped
1 tablespoon chopped parsley

Brown the chicken pieces as directed under Basic Chicken Sauté (page 4) and season. Reduce the heat and add the onion and garlic. Cover and cook for 5 minutes. Add the wine, cover, and cook for 10 minutes. Add the tomatoes, cover, and cook 10 minutes more. Remove the chicken to a hot platter. Add parsley to the sauce and let it cook down for a minute or so. Correct the seasoning and pour over the chicken.

Serves four.

A LEMON SAUTÉ

6 tablespoons butter
1 broiler-fryer, 3½ pounds, quartered
Salt and freshly ground black pepper
Juice of 2 lemons
Finely grated zest of 1 lemon
1 tablespoon chopped parsley

~ Heat the butter in a heavy skillet and brown the chicken pieces. Season to taste, reduce the heat, and cover. Cook very gently for about 25 minutes, turning twice.

Just before removing the cooked chicken from the pan, pour the lemon juice and zest over it. Cook for a minute, sprinkle with chopped parsley, and remove to a hot platter. Pour the pan juices over it.

During asparagus season, serve this dish with cooked asparagus lightly dusted with Parmesan cheese, arranging it around the chicken on the platter. You might also serve tiny new potatoes with chopped chives, and crusty French bread.

Serves four.

A SAUTÉ WITH MUSHROOMS

2 broilers, 2 pounds each, split
Flour for dredging
Salt and freshly ground black pepper
4 tablespoons butter or other fat
1 tablespoon chopped onion
1 cup tiny mushroom caps or sliced mushrooms

Dredge the chicken halves with flour, salt, and pepper. Melt the butter or other fat in one very large skillet or two smaller ones and brown the chicken well on all sides. Reduce the heat and add the onion and the mushroom caps or sliced mushrooms. Cover the pan or pans and simmer for 10 minutes. Uncover, turn the chicken, and cook till tender. Correct the seasoning and arrange on a hot platter with the mushrooms and pan juices poured around it. Serve with fresh peas and a tossed green salad.

Serves four.

CHICKEN BASQUAISE

6 tablespoons unsalted butter

2 frying chickens, 2 to 2½ pounds each, quartered

Salt and freshly ground pepper

¾ cup dry white wine

3 tablespoons olive oil

1 medium onion, finely chopped

2 green peppers, seeded and cut in 1-inch squares

2 canned green chilies, chopped

1½ cups canned Italian plum tomatoes, drained

¼ cup cognac

Pinch of saffron

¼ pound Virginia ham, diced

Chopped parsley

Brown the chicken in the butter in a heavy sauté pan. Reduce the heat, sprinkle with salt and pepper, and cover with a tight-fitting lid. Cook gently 5 to 8 minutes. Add ¼ cup of wine and cook another 10 minutes. Move the breast pieces to the top—the dark meat will take longer to cook—and continue cooking for 5 to 10 minutes, until just tender.

Meanwhile, prepare the sauce. Heat the olive oil in a skillet, add the onion, peppers, and chilies, and cook until soft. Add the tomatoes, cognac, remaining wine, and saffron. Simmer, uncovered, until reduced and thickened. Add the ham. Taste for seasoning. Pour the sauce over the chicken and sprinkle with chopped parsley. Serve with saffron rice.

Serves four.

A SAUTÉ WITH PEPPERS

4 or 5 green or red sweet peppers
2 small broilers or 1 large fryer, 3½ pounds in all
Flour for dredging
Salt and freshly ground black pepper
⅔ cup olive oil or cooking oil
2 tablespoons chopped onion
1 clove garlic, finely chopped
2 large tomatoes, peeled, seeded, and finely chopped
Lemon juice to taste
1 tablespoon chopped parsley

❧ Broil the green or red peppers till skins are blackened and loosened from the flesh. Remove the skins and seeds and cut into strips. Set aside.

Prepare chicken for sauté. Dredge with flour, salt, and pepper. Heat the olive oil or cooking oil in one large, heavy skillet or two smaller ones and brown the chicken, turning frequently to get an evenness of color. Reduce the heat, add the onion and garlic, cover, and cook for 10 minutes. Add the tomatoes and let cook down for about 5 minutes, turning the chicken in the sauce several times. Add the pepper strips and heat through. Correct the seasoning, and just before serving add a few drops of lemon juice and the chopped parsley. This is excellent with polenta.

Serves four.

A SAUTÉ WITH ONIONS

2 large Spanish onions, thinly sliced
7 tablespoons butter
3 tablespoons vegetable oil
1 fryer, 3½ pounds, cut up

Salt and freshly ground black pepper, to taste

Place the thinly sliced onions in a heavy-bottomed skillet over low heat and stir until they begin to color. Then add 4 tablespoons butter and allow to brown. Meanwhile, in another large skillet, melt 3 tablespoons butter with the oil. Brown the dark meat over fairly high heat. Add the white meat and brown, then add the browned onions. Add salt and pepper to taste. Cover the pan and simmer for 12 to 15 minutes, or until the chicken is tender. Arrange on a hot platter with the onions and serve with sautéed potatoes and a green salad.

Serves four.

A SAUTÉ WITH CABBAGE

2 broilers, 2 pounds each, split
Flour for dredging
9 tablespoons butter
Salt and freshly ground black pepper
1 medium head cabbage, shredded
1½ teaspoons caraway seeds
1 cup heavy cream

🥄 Flour the chicken. Heat 6 tablespoons butter in one very large skillet or two smaller ones and brown the chicken. Add salt and pepper to taste and continue cooking for about 10 minutes.

Meanwhile, wash the shredded cabbage. Cook in 2 cups salted water till almost tender, about 5 minutes. Drain and toss with 3 tablespoons butter and the caraway seeds. Add to the chicken. Pour the cream over, cover, and let simmer for 10 to 15 minutes. Taste for seasoning and serve.

Serves four.

A SAUTÉ WITH HAM

6 tablespoons butter
2 small broilers or 1 large fryer, 3½ pounds in all, cut up
2 thin slices smoked ham, cut into julienne
1 medium onion, very finely chopped
1 large clove garlic, grated
1 cup sliced mushrooms
Several sprigs of parsley, coarsely chopped
Salt and freshly ground black pepper
½ cup white wine

🥄 Melt the butter in one large, heavy skillet or two smaller ones. Add the chicken pieces and brown on all sides. Reduce the heat and add the smoked ham, onion, and garlic. Sauté for 10 minutes. Add the mushrooms and parsley. Turn the chicken; add salt and pepper to taste. Cover and cook another 10 to 12 minutes, or till tender. About 5 minutes before the chicken is done, add the white wine and let it cook down. Remove the chicken to a hot platter and pour the sauce over it. Serve with corn pudding or spoon bread.

Serves four.

A SAUTÉ WITH OYSTERS

4 tablespoons butter
4 to 6 chicken legs with thighs
Salt and freshly ground black pepper
Flour for dredging
18 oysters, shucked and liquor reserved
2 egg yolks, beaten
1½ to 2 cups cracker crumbs, or as needed
1 cup clarified butter, or as needed
¼ cup sherry
Chopped parsley

Heat the 4 tablespoons of butter in a skillet and brown the chicken over a brisk flame. Add salt and pepper to taste. Cover and sauté till tender, about 15 to 20 minutes.

While the chicken is cooking, flour the oysters and dip in beaten egg yolk, then in cracker crumbs, and fry in ½ inch clarified butter till nicely browned. Season to taste. Remove the chicken and oysters from their pans and arrange on a hot platter. Add the oyster liquor to the oyster pan and heat it well, scraping the residue from the pan into the sauce. Add this, along with the sherry, to the pan in which the chicken was cooked and let it cook down for a minute or two. Pour over the chicken and oysters, sprinkle with chopped parsley, and serve.

Serves four.

A SAUTÉ WITH CURRY AND TOMATO SAUCE

3 tablespoons butter
1 broiler, 2 pounds, split
Salt and freshly ground black pepper
1 medium onion, very finely chopped
1 cup fresh tomato purée
1 tablespoon curry powder or to taste

⋙ Melt the butter in a heavy skillet and brown the chicken over brisk heat. Reduce the heat, add salt and pepper to taste and the onion. Cover and cook until the chicken is tender, about 20 to 25 minutes. Remove to a hot platter or casserole.

Add the tomato purée and curry powder to the pan juices and let it cook down for several minutes, stirring to create a good blend. Taste for seasoning. Pour steaming hot over the chicken, and serve with boiled rice and a little chutney.

Serves two.

A VIENNESE SAUTÉ

1 chicken, 2 pounds, quartered
3 tablespoons clarified butter or other fat
1 tablespoon chopped onion
2 tablespoons paprika
Salt and freshly ground black pepper to taste
½ cup heavy cream
½ cup chicken broth
1 tablespoon butter
Dash of lemon juice
Chopped parsley

Prepare the chicken for sauté. Cook very gently in the clarified butter or other fat until delicately browned. Add the onion, paprika, and salt and pepper and cook until well blended. Reduce the heat, cover, and simmer gently for 20 to 25 minutes. Remove the chicken to a hot platter. Add to the pan the cream and the chicken broth, which can be made from the giblets. Then add 1 tablespoon butter and let the sauce reduce over brisk heat for 3 to 4 minutes. Finally add a dash of lemon juice and a sprinkling of parsley. Pour the sauce around the chicken. Serve with thin slices of zucchini sautéed in garlic and olive oil.

Serves two.

A SOUTHWESTERN SAUTÉ

This is a purely American Southwest version of the sauté, and one that has a delicious tang. I had it first at the home of a friend in Arizona. It was served with a large dish of polenta, made with water-ground cornmeal flavored with butter and grated Parmesan cheese. We washed it all down with a bottle of rough, rich claret.

2 broilers or fryers, 2 pounds each, quartered
6 to 8 thin slices of bacon
Flour for dredging
Salt and freshly ground black pepper to taste
2 teaspoons paprika
Sprinkle of cayenne
2 cloves garlic, finely chopped
1 small white onion, finely chopped
1 cup tomato purée
2 teaspoons chili powder
Sweet basil, fresh or dried, to taste
⅓ cup dry red wine
Chopped parsley

Prepare chickens for sauté. Fry the bacon in a large skillet till crisp and free of most of the fat. Remove the bacon and keep warm. Dredge the chicken with flour and brown it quickly in the hot bacon fat. Add salt and pepper, the paprika, cayenne, garlic, and onion. Reduce the heat, cover, and cook for 10 minutes. Then add the tomato purée, chili powder, and sweet basil to taste. Allow this to simmer for another 10 minutes, or until the chicken is tender. Remove to a hot platter. Add the red wine to the pan juices and cook down for 3 minutes. Taste for seasoning. Pour the sauce over the chicken, sprinkle with chopped parsley, and garnish with the bacon.

Serves four.

CHICKEN BREASTS WITH MUSHROOM SAUCE

3 whole chicken breasts, cut in half, skinned, and boned
Salt and freshly ground black pepper
Lemon juice to taste
Flour for dredging
2 eggs, lightly beaten
1½ to 2 cups bread crumbs made from crustless day-old French bread
4 tablespoons butter, more if needed
3 tablespoons olive oil
¾ pound small, whole mushrooms
¼ cup Madeira
¾ cup heavy cream
1 egg yolk
¼ teaspoon ground allspice

Flatten the chicken breasts slightly between two sheets of waxed paper and season lightly with salt, pepper, and lemon juice. Flour the pieces, dip into the lightly beaten egg, then coat with the bread crumbs. Put on a plate and chill for 1 hour.

Heat the butter and oil in a large skillet and sauté the breasts over moderately low heat for 3 minutes on each side, or until they are just cooked through and browned. Transfer the breasts to a hot platter and keep them warm. In the same skillet sauté the mushrooms for 2 to 3 minutes, or until browned, adding more butter if necessary. Using a slotted spoon, transfer the mushrooms to a dish. Pour the fat from the skillet and add the Madeira. Reduce the liquid by half over high heat, scraping in the brown bits clinging to the bottom and sides of the pan.

In a bowl, combine the heavy cream, egg yolk, ¼ teaspoon salt, allspice, and pepper to taste. Gradually stir the cream mixture into the reduced liquid over low heat. Do not allow to boil. Add the reserved mushrooms and continue to cook the sauce over low heat, stirring until thickened. Pour the sauce over the breasts and serve with saffron rice.

Serves six.

CHICKEN BREASTS ARMAGNAC

2 whole chicken breasts, halved, with wings attached
6 tablespoons butter
Salt and freshly ground black pepper
6 to 8 shallots, peeled and chopped extremely fine
2 egg yolks
¾ cup heavy cream
⅓ cup Armagnac

Brown the chicken in the butter in a heavy skillet. Add salt and pepper and continue to cook for about 10 to 12 minutes, turning the pieces frequently. When done, transfer to a hot platter.

Add the shallots to the skillet and cook until tender. Reduce heat and slowly add the egg yolks and cream, beaten together. Cook over low heat, stirring constantly, until thoroughly blended and thickened; do not allow to boil.

Set the skillet aside. Heat the Armagnac and quickly pour it over the chicken; flambé. When the Armagnac is almost burned out, pour the sauce around the chicken. Serve with rice pilaf.

Serves four.

CHICKEN YUCATAN

2 whole chicken breasts, cut in half, or 4 thighs and legs

Flour for dredging

3 tablespoons butter

3 tablespoons olive oil

Salt and freshly ground black pepper

⅓ cup Cognac

1 can (6 ounces) undiluted, frozen concentrated orange juice

1 can (4 ounces) peeled green chilies, drained and finely chopped

1 clove garlic, finely chopped

½ cup pine nuts

¼ cup dried currants or sultana raisins

Chopped parsley

🐦 Remove the rib bones from the chicken breasts, if using, and trim them neatly. Dust lightly with flour. Heat the butter and oil in a skillet and lightly sear the chicken on both sides until ivory colored. Add salt and pepper to taste. Warm the Cognac, pour over the chicken, and flambé. Add the orange juice concentrate, chilies, and garlic. Simmer for approximately 10 minutes, or until the chicken is just tender. Turn several times during the cooking. Remove to a hot platter.

Let the sauce cook down for a minute. Pour over the chicken and sprinkle with the pine nuts, currants, and chopped parsley. Serve with rice.

Serves four.

CHICKEN LEGS WITH YOGURT

6 chicken legs
3 tablespoons oil
3 tablespoons butter
Salt and freshly ground black pepper
1 cup chicken broth
½ cup yogurt
2 red bell peppers, roasted, peeled, seeded and cut in ½ inch strips

❧ Brown the chicken on all sides in the oil and butter. Season with salt and pepper. Add the broth and simmer until tender, 20 to 25 minutes, turning once or twice. Remove the chicken to a warm platter. Reduce the pan juices by half over high heat. Remove the pan from the heat and stir in the yogurt. Gently reheat, but do not allow to boil. Add the pepper strips, taste for seasoning, and pour over the chicken.

Serves six.

CHICKEN LEGS WITH PAPRIKA AND SOUR CREAM

6 chicken legs
3 tablespoons oil
3 tablespoons butter
1½ cups chopped onions
1 tablespoon paprika
1 cup chicken broth
1 cup sour cream
1 tablespoon grated lemon rind

Brown the chicken in the oil and butter, and transfer to a platter. Add the onions to the pan, and sauté until lightly colored. Stir in the paprika and cook another 1 or 2 minutes. Return the chicken to the pan, add the broth, and simmer until tender, 20 to 25 minutes. Remove the chicken to a serving platter. Stir the sour cream into the pan juices. Gently reheat but do not allow to boil. Pour over the chicken, and sprinkle with the lemon rind.

Serves six.

SAUTÉED CHICKEN WINGS

4 tablespoons butter
1 pound chicken wings
Salt and freshly ground black pepper to taste

Heat the butter in a heavy skillet. Add the chicken wings and sauté gently for 12 to 15 minutes, turning often. Add salt and pepper and cover the pan for about 10 minutes. Serve with new potatoes and green peas.

Serves two to three.

Variations

1. Sauté 5 or 6 bacon strips, remove, and add the wings to the bacon fat. Proceed as above. Garnish with the bacon.
2. Add 2 medium onions, finely chopped, to the sauté. When the wings are well browned, add 1 cup tomato sauce, 1 tablespoon chopped parsley, a pinch of dried thyme, and 3 or 4 pitted olives, cut in thin slices. Simmer, covered, for 15 minutes. Serve with rice.
3. Add 2 teaspoons paprika to the sauté. Just before serving, add ½ cup heavy cream and blend well.

SAUTÉED SQUAB CHICKENS

    6 tablespoons butter
    2 tablespoons olive oil
    4 squab chickens, about 1 pound each, split
    Salt and freshly ground black pepper
    ½ cup Cognac or Madeira
    4 tablespoons chopped parsley

🐦 You will need two large skillets to do this at one time. Divide the butter and oil between the skillets and heat until bubbling. Place the chickens in the skillets, skin side down, and brown nicely over high heat. Sprinkle with salt and pepper, turn, and reduce the heat to medium. Cook for another 12 to 15 minutes. Test with a fork to see if the juices run clear. The birds should be done in 18 to 20 minutes, in all. Transfer to a hot platter. Rinse each skillet with ¼ cup of Cognac or Madeira, and stir in the chopped parsley. Pour over the chicken.

Serves four to eight.

JOHN BEARD'S SAUTÉED CHICKEN

My father, who came of stalwart pioneer stock—he crossed the continent to Oregon in a covered wagon when he was five—had many definite ideas about food and life. Not only did he have the ideas, but he worked at them with a vengeance. One of them, which became a tradition in our home, must have had its influence on me at an early age.

    Father felt that he could sauté a chicken better than anyone else in the family, in fact better than anyone else he had ever known. He liked a young chicken sautéed for Sunday morning breakfast. So, early on Sunday—Father was never a late sleeper—he could be found in the kitchen complete with chicken, utensils, and apron. No one dared set foot in the "domestic offices" till the chicken was in the pan and wafting its glorious aroma throughout the lower floor of the house. He never would keep doors closed.

Father cut the chickens, or chicken, in ten pieces and dredged them lightly with flour. He then cut several slices of bacon from "the side" (don't think for one minute that sliced bacon was ever allowed in his house) and cut it in thin strips. These were fried out over a slow fire so that they became crisp and left a good deal of delicious fat in the iron skillet. The strips were removed to a platter, which was heating, and the pieces of chicken were lovingly lowered into the hot bacon fat. These he seared quickly, turning them and arranging them in the pan so that each morsel received the same degree of brownness and crispness.

Then the pan was covered, the flame turned low, and the chicken simmered for about 15 minutes. The cover was then removed and the pieces allowed just a few more minutes to take on additional crispness before being transferred to a hot platter.

Next came another rite: a heaping tablespoon of flour was put in the pan, after all the excess grease had been poured off, and was blended thoroughly with the little bits of goodness left in the pan. When these bits had been scraped around and melted with the flour, 2 cups of rich milk were poured in, the careful stirring began, and the seasoning was added, to Father's taste. He loved freshly ground black pepper and seemed to have a magic touch with it, for no one else I know has ever made it blend and yet retain its individuality the way Father did. When the sauce had achieved the proper degree of thickness for him, it was transferred to a hot bowl and breakfast was announced.

Of course, I neglected to say that he admitted someone else to the kitchen in time to make a huge pan of crispy hot biscuits or an iron pan filled with magnificent popovers. But I am not discussing baking in this book.

Need I add that friends of the family and of mine were always pleased to stay overnight at our house?

Fried Chicken

Though its origins go back to English and Viennese cooking, fried chicken has become a distinctively American tradition, especially in the South, where it was transformed into a great Creole specialty. The ease with which it can be prepared, and the increasing abundance of chicken, has made it one of our most ubiquitous and most popular national dishes, found at drive-ins, quick-food chain restaurants, and small local restaurants from coast to coast.

Our renowned Southern-fried chicken, which is often really sautéed rather than fried, comes in many forms, variously known as chicken Maryland, Virginia fried chicken, or Creole fried chicken. Essentially a very simple dish, its success depends on the care with which it is cooked. It can be floured, breaded, or dipped in batter; and the cooking can be done in lard, lard and butter, or vegetable oil. Whatever the variation, the chicken must have a crisp golden-brown coating and a juicy interior, while absorbing a minimum of cooking fat.

CREOLE FRIED CHICKEN

1 fryer, 3 to 3½ pounds, cut into 8 pieces
Lemon juice
2 eggs
⅓ cup milk
Flour for dredging
Rolled cracker crumbs
Lard or cooking oil for deep frying
Salt and freshly ground black pepper

Rub the chicken well with lemon juice. Beat the eggs with the milk, coat the chicken with the mixture, and let stand for 1 to 1½ hours. Then roll each piece in flour and cracker crumbs and drop into enough medium-hot lard or cooking oil to cover the chicken completely. Cook for 15 to 18 minutes or until the chicken is well browned. Season with salt and pepper to taste and drain on paper towels.

Serves four.

CHICKEN MARYLAND

There are countless recipes for this dish, and which is the original I cannot tell you. Escoffier, in his book *Ma Cuisine*, calls for a chicken to be floured, coated with egg and bread crumbs, and cooked in clarified butter until golden brown. This is put on a serving plate with sweet corn fritters, potato croquettes, bacon and banana, and served with a béchamel sauce to which a little horseradish has been added. M. Escoffier also suggests serving the dish with a tomato sauce!

A more authentic source, a very old Maryland and Virginia cookbook, says the chicken should be dredged with flour and cooked in a skillet in boiling lard about 2½ inches deep and served with a gravy made with drippings from the chicken, flour, milk, and salt and pepper—this to be served with rice. The most delicious dish I have ever eaten under the name of chicken Maryland had a crisp crust on it and was served with a smooth cream gravy and corn fritters. Here is a version that I have found successful.

2 broilers, 2 pounds each, split
Lemon juice
2 eggs, beaten
Salt and freshly ground black pepper
1 cup milk
½ pound bacon, cut up
1½ to 2 cups dried bread crumbs
2 tablespoons flour
2 cups half-and-half or milk and cream mixed

Rub the chickens well with lemon juice and place in a batter made of the beaten eggs, a little salt and pepper, and the milk. Turn to coat all sides and let stand for 2 hours.

Cook the bacon in a skillet till crisp. Remove the bacon. Dip the soaked chicken pieces in the finely rolled bread crumbs and brown quickly in the hot bacon fat, turning to color evenly. Reduce the heat and cook till tender, about 10 to 12 minutes. Season with salt and pepper to taste.

Remove the chicken from the pan and pour off all the fat except 2 tablespoons. Add the flour, blend with the fat, and cook for 2 or 3 minutes. Add the half-and-half and stir till thickened and smooth. Add salt and pepper to taste.

The traditional way to serve this dish is to arrange the chicken in a bed of the cream sauce and garnish with strips of bacon and corn fritters.

Serves four.

Variation

Prepare the chicken as above.

Heat cooking oil or fat in a deep frying kettle to 370°F. Place the chicken in the frying basket and immerse in the hot fat. Unless you have a huge kettle, it is wise to cook one or two pieces at a time. The entire chicken should cook in 8 to 11 minutes, according to weight and size.

Drain on paper towels and serve with a rich béchamel sauce (see page 237) and corn fritters.

VIRGINIA FRIED CHICKEN WITH BROWNED GRAVY

This recipe comes from Edna Lewis's book, *A Taste of Country Cooking*.

1 cup all-purpose unbleached flour
1 cup whole-wheat flour
1 tablespoon salt
1 teaspoon freshly ground black pepper
2 chickens, 2¼ to 2½ pounds each, cut into 8 pieces each
½ cup lard, at room temperature
8 tablespoons butter, at room temperature
1 slice smoked ham, cut in julienne (optional)

❧ Combine the two flours and add the salt and pepper; mix well. After the chickens have been rinsed and cut into serving pieces, wipe them lightly with a damp cloth. Reserve the backs and wing tips for the stock, which should be started at this point (see page 29). Roll each piece of chicken in the flour mixture and place the coated pieces on a wide platter or a sheet of waxed paper. Leave the floured pieces to rest for an hour or so to allow time for the flour to adhere to the chicken, avoiding loose flour falling into the frying pan.

To fry the chicken, heat the skillet hot and add the lard. When the lard nearly begins to smoke, add chicken pieces, butter, and ham. Cover and cook on a brisk flame, to a good golden color, 10 to 12 minutes on each side. Remove the cooked pieces from the skillet, drain on paper towels, and serve piping hot with gravy.

Serves five to six.

Gravy

3 chicken backs, plus any wing tips and feet
1 stalk celery with leaves
1 thick slice onion
3 cups cold water
Fat from the skillet
3 rounded tablespoons flour
Salt and freshly ground black pepper

◆ Prepare the stock in advance with the chicken backs, celery, onion, and water in a saucepan. Put on a medium burner to cook for 1 hour, gently but continuously. When cooked enough, strain and set aside to cool and skim off the fat. When the chicken is halfway through cooking, spoon out about 4 or 5 tablespoons of fat from the pan in which it is cooking into a 9-inch skillet, add the flour, and set over a medium flame. Stir until the pan heats up and the flour turns a dark chestnut brown. Remove the skillet from the burner and add 2½ cups chicken stock. Stir well and return the skillet to the burner. Bring to a simmer and cook gently for 15 minutes. Season to taste with salt and pepper. If the gravy is too thick, add more stock or plain water. Remove any excess fat that rises to the top of the gravy.

PAN-FRIED CHICKEN

1 fryer, 2½ to 3 pounds, cut into 8 pieces
Flour for dredging
Salt and freshly ground black pepper
Lard for frying
1 cup heavy cream, blended with 2 egg yolks

🐦 Dredge the chicken pieces heavily with flour, salt, and pepper. Let stand on a rack for 30 minutes or longer. Melt ½ to ¾ inch of lard in a skillet, and when it is very hot, brown the chicken pieces quickly on all sides. Do not crowd the pan. If necessary, brown a few pieces at a time and transfer to a platter lined with paper towels in a 300°F oven while you continue cooking. When all the chicken is browned, arrange in the skillet, reduce the heat, and cover. Allow to cook for 20 to 25 minutes. After 10 minutes, rearrange the pieces to bring the white meat to the top; and after 15 to 20 minutes, remove the white meat to a hot platter and keep warm.

When all the chicken is done, remove from the pan and pour off all but 1 tablespoon fat. Add the cream mixed with the egg yolks and stir over low heat till thickened; do not allow to boil. Season to taste. Pour over the chicken and serve at once.

Serves four.

Variation

Clay Triplette's Pan-Fried Chicken: Dredge the chicken with flour, 1 teaspoon salt, 1 teaspoon freshly ground black pepper, and ¼ teaspoon cinnamon. Brown on all sides in 1 cup shortening, reduce the heat, and cook for 10 minutes. Cover, and cook the white meat for 5 minutes more, the dark meat for 10 minutes.

CHICKEN KIEV

12 tablespoons butter

2 tablespoons chopped parsley

1½ teaspoons dried tarragon

1 clove garlic, finely chopped

Salt and freshly ground black pepper to taste

6 whole chicken breasts, cut in half, boned, and skinned

Seasoned flour for dredging

2 eggs, beaten

1 to 1½ cups fresh bread crumbs

Cooking oil or clarified butter for deep frying

Soften the butter in a bowl and mix with the herbs, garlic, and seasonings. Form into 12 fingers and freeze until firm, about 45 minutes.

Wash the chicken breasts and pat dry. With a mallet or meat pounder, flatten the breasts between two sheets of waxed paper. Place a finger of butter in the center of each chicken piece. Roll the chicken around the butter, tucking in the ends to seal well. Roll each breast in seasoned flour. Dip into beaten egg, and then into bread crumbs to coat. Place on a piece of foil and freeze or chill for 1 hour. To cook, fry the breasts in deep oil or clarified butter for about 5 to 6 minutes, or until crisp and brown. Drain and serve immediately.

Serves twelve.

STUFFED BREAST OF CHICKEN WITH MUSHROOM SAUCE

This is a recipe from the files of one of America's famous restaurant chains, Schrafft's. It makes a good dish for a dinner party or buffet.

4 whole chicken breasts, cut in half, boned, and poached in butter
3 cups sliced mushroom caps, sautéed (reserve the stems)
1½ tablespoons finely chopped onion
2 tablespoons chopped parsley
¼ cup dried bread crumbs
¼ cup heavy cream
Salt and freshly ground black pepper
Flour for dredging
Finely rolled cracker crumbs
2 eggs, beaten
Fresh bread crumbs
10 tablespoons clarified butter for frying

For the Sauce

8 tablespoons butter
½ cup flour
½ cup milk, scalded
¼ cup heavy cream
2 cups rich chicken stock
¼ cup or more Madeira

꙾ Cut a pocket in each of the cooked chicken breasts. Prepare a filling with two-thirds of the sautéed mushrooms, the onion, parsley, dried bread crumbs, heavy cream, and salt and pepper to taste. Stuff the breasts with this mixture.

Flour the stuffed breasts, roll in fine cracker crumbs, dip in beaten egg seasoned with salt and pepper, and finally roll in fresh bread crumbs. Quickly brown in clarified butter.

Prepare the sauce: Cook the reserved mushroom stems in water to cover for 10 minutes. Strain and set aside. Melt the butter in a saucepan, and blend in the flour. Cook for a minute or two, then add the scalded milk, heavy cream, and chicken stock. Cook, stirring constantly, till well thickened. Add ½ cup of reserved mushroom liquor, the remaining sautéed mushrooms, and the Madeira. Correct the seasoning. Stir until blended and heated through.

Serves eight.

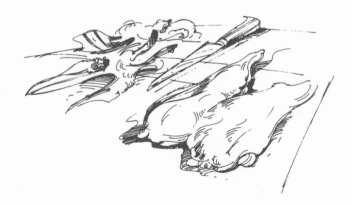

SAUTÉED STUFFED CHICKEN BREASTS

3 whole chicken breasts, boned, skinned, and cut in half
¼ pound mushrooms, finely chopped
2 tablespoons finely chopped shallots
6 tablespoons butter
Salt and freshly ground black pepper
Flour
3 tablespoons peanut or olive oil
¾ cup dry white wine or dry vermouth
2 tablespoons chopped parsley

Flatten each chicken breast half between sheets of waxed paper. Sauté the mushrooms and shallots in 3 tablespoons butter over medium heat until the mixture darkens and loses its moisture, 12 to 15 minutes. Season well with salt and pepper to taste.

Put a tablespoon of the mushroom mixture on one half of each chicken breast and fold over the other half. Secure with a skewer or toothpick. Dust with flour, then sauté in the oil and remaining butter over medium heat, about 4 minutes on each side, until lightly brown. Remove to a warm dish. Add ½ cup of wine to the pan, and let it cook down for a minute while you scrape loose any residue. Return the breasts to the pan, lower the heat to a simmer, and cook, covered, for 3 minutes on each side. Test for doneness; the breasts should be cooked through but still moist. Remove again to a warm dish. Spoon off excess fat from the pan juices, then add the remaining wine to the pan and cook for a few seconds. Pour the sauce over the breasts, sprinkle with parsley, and serve.

Serves four to six.

CHICKEN PANNÉ

4 whole chicken breasts, cut in half and boned
Flour
2 eggs, beaten
Fresh bread crumbs
6 tablespoons butter
Salt and freshly ground black pepper
3 tablespoons Cognac, warmed
1 cup cream, blended with 2 egg yolks

❧ Put the boned breasts between two sheets of waxed paper and pound quite flat with a heavy cleaver or meat pounder. Dip in the flour, beaten egg, and bread crumbs, in that order. Refrigerate until ready to use.

To cook, heat the butter in a skillet over a high flame until bubbling, but not smoking. Add the chicken breasts, two at a time, and brown quickly for a few minutes on both sides, sprinkling with salt and pepper, and transferring to a hot platter as they are done. Return to the pan and, off-heat, flame with the Cognac. Remove to the hot platter and keep warm. To the skillet, add the cream-egg mixture and stir over medium heat until just thickened, making sure it does not come to a boil. Correct the seasoning and serve with the chicken.

Serves eight.

Variation

For a less rich dish, serve without the sauce and with just a squeeze of lemon.

Poached Chicken

Poached chicken can be a delicious dish, especially when it is treated like the *poule au pot* of France or the *pollo bollito* of Italy. But it requires careful simmering—the merest bubbling. If you allow it to boil away, you will have overcooked meat and all the flavor will have drained into the broth. Remove the chicken when it is just tender and cook the broth down for a richer flavor. If you stuff the bird, be sure the vent is well sewn up and covered or the broth will seep in and make the stuffing soggy.

Poached chicken can be served either hot or cold. If serving cold, allow it to cool to room temperature. It will taste far better than if it has been touched by the rigor mortis of refrigeration.

POACHED CHICKEN WITH DUMPLINGS

1 roasting chicken, 5 to 6 pounds
½ lemon
Several sprigs of parsley
1 bay leaf
1 medium onion, stuck with 2 or 3 cloves
8 peppercorns
Dash of freshly grated nutmeg
Salt to taste
Cold water to cover
Either of the two dumpling recipes that follow
Chopped parsley

🌱 Rub the chicken, inside and out, with the half-lemon. Put the parsley sprigs in the cavity of the chicken and truss (see page 57). Place in a deep kettle with the bay leaf, onion, peppercorns, nutmeg, and salt to taste. Cover with cold water, place over medium-high heat, and bring to a boil. Remove the scum, reduce the heat, and cover tightly. Simmer until tender, about 45 to 60 minutes. Do not overcook or you will have a stringy mess. Remove the chicken to a hot platter and keep warm. Strain the broth, return to the pot, and let it cook down over high heat. Then cook the dumplings in the broth. You may serve the broth first, followed by the chicken and dumplings, both sprinkled with chopped parsley.

Serves four to six.

Light Dumplings
  2 cups flour
  4½ teaspoons baking powder
  ¼ teaspoon salt
  1 cup milk

Sift together the flour and baking powder. Combine all the ingredients and toss together lightly with a fork. Drop by spoonfuls into boiling broth. Cover the pan tightly and allow to cook for 13 minutes to the dot.

Nellie Cox's Dumplings
Nellie Cox belonged to the American school of cookery that created hearty, honest food.

  2 cups flour
  2 tablespoons butter
  Salt to taste
  Water as needed

Mix the flour, butter, and salt, adding enough water to make a stiff dough. Roll out to the thickness of ⅛ inch. Cut in pieces 1 x 3 inches. Drop into boiling broth and cook for 20 minutes, uncovered, stirring frequently to keep them from sticking.

POACHED CHICKEN WITH RICE

1 large roasting chicken, 4 to 5 pounds
½ lemon
1 onion, stuck with 3 cloves
Few sprigs of parsley
1 carrot
Pinch of dried thyme
Cold water to cover
Salt to taste
1 cup raw rice

Rub the chicken, inside and out, with the half-lemon. Put the onion, parsley, carrot, and thyme in the cavity of the chicken and truss (see page 57). Place in a deep kettle, cover with cold water, and bring to a boil. Remove the scum, then reduce the heat, add salt to taste, and cover tightly. Simmer until just tender, about 50 to 60 minutes. Remove the chicken and cook down the broth. Before doing so, draw off 2 cups of the broth. Combine with the rice in a small, heavy pot, cover, and simmer for 15 minutes, or until tender. (The rice can also be cooked in the pot while the broth reduces.) Return the chicken to the kettle and correct the seasoning. Serve with the rice and broth.

Serves four.

CHICKEN IN THE POT

This is a version of the French dish known to the world as *poule au pot*. It is the custom in France to drink bowls of the broth followed by the chicken.

1 large roasting chicken, 4 to 5 pounds, liver and gizzard reserved
½ lemon
½ pound sausage meat
2 medium onions, finely chopped
1 medium clove garlic, chopped
1½ cups dry bread crumbs
1 tablespoon chopped parsley
Pinch of dried thyme
Salt and freshly ground black pepper to taste
6 egg yolks, beaten
Crust of old bread
1 pound beef shin
1 pound veal neck
Salt pork or bacon
Cold water to cover

Rub the interior of the chicken with half a lemon. Stuff it with the following mixture:

Fry the sausage meat in a skillet till it is rendered of its fat. Pour off most of the fat and add the onions and garlic. Let this cook a few minutes before adding the bread crumbs. Mix well and add the reserved liver and gizzard chopped, and the parsley, thyme, and salt and pepper. Remove from the heat and let cool. Add the beaten egg yolks. Mix thoroughly with the hands and stuff the bird, but not too tightly. Place a crust of old bread over the vent and sew it up securely. Tie the neck skin and truss the bird (see page 57). Place in a large pot with beef shin, veal neck, and a small piece of salt pork or bacon (see variation). Cover with cold water, bring to a boil, and skim. Reduce the heat, cover, and simmer till the chicken is tender, about 50 to 60 minutes. Remove the chicken to cool. Reduce the broth by one-third until you have one that is rich and strong. Skim off the fat. Serve the hot broth in bowls, and follow with the cooled chicken and the stuffing, which may be removed and sliced. Serve with a good mustard mayonnaise and salad.

Serves four.

Variation

Carrots and onions may be added to the broth while it is cooking, and then may be served with the soup. You may also flavor the broth with parsley, thyme, and rosemary.

POACHED CHICKEN FARM STYLE

1 large boiling fowl, 4 to 5 pounds
½ lemon
Stuffing of your choice (see pages 227-236)
Crust of old bread
Cold water to cover
6 medium onions, peeled
6 to 8 carrots
A sprig or two of parsley
Salt and freshly ground black pepper
6 to 8 small turnips, peeled
Potatoes, peeled
1 cup heavy cream, blended with 2 egg yolks

Rub the fowl, inside and out, with the half-lemon. Remove the fowl's wing ends, but add to the pot. Fill the chicken with the stuffing of your choice and sew up the vent securely, having covered the stuffing with an old crust of bread before closing the vent. Sew up the skin at the neck end of the bird and fasten securely with a skewer. Truss. Place in a kettle with cold water to cover. Bring to a boil, skim, and reduce the heat. Cover tightly and simmer 1 hour. Add the onions, carrots, a sprig or two of parsley, and salt to taste and continue simmering for another 1 to 1½ hours. Then add the turnips and 1 or 2 potatoes per person. When tender, remove chicken and continue cooking the vegetables till they are done.

Remove 2 cups of the broth, strain and degrease and combine with the cream and egg yolks. Stir over low heat till well thickened, but do not allow to boil. Add salt and pepper to taste. Place chicken on a hot platter and remove all strings and skewers. Arrange the vegetables around it and serve with the sauce.

Serves four.

POACHED CHICKEN WITH SPAGHETTI

1 large roasting chicken, about 5 or 6 pounds

½ lemon

1 onion, stuck with 3 cloves

3 sprigs parsley

1 sprig fresh thyme

3 leaves fresh sweet basil

Cold water to cover

Salt and freshly ground black pepper

1 large onion, finely chopped

2 cloves garlic, chopped

2 tablespoons butter

2 cans (each 1 pound) Italian tomatoes

2 tablespoons chopped parsley

1½ pounds spaghetti

Freshly grated Parmesan cheese

Rub the interior of the chicken with half a lemon. Fill the cavity with the onion stuck with the cloves, 3 parsley sprigs, thyme sprig, and 2 leaves of sweet basil. Cover with cold water; bring to a boil and skim. Salt and pepper to taste, reduce heat, cover, and simmer until tender, about 50 to 60 minutes. Remove the meat from the bones and reserve; return the carcass to the pot and simmer till the broth is reduced by half.

Sauté the chopped onion and garlic in the butter. Add the Italian tomatoes and cook down until thickened. Add the remaining basil and 2 tablespoons chopped parsley. Season with salt and pepper to taste. Mix this with the chicken meat, and add the chicken broth after removing the carcass. Simmer over a very low flame for 30 minutes.

Cook the spaghetti in boiling, salted water till al dente. Drain and remove to a large bowl. Ladle the sauce and chicken over the pasta and sprinkle liberally with Parmesan cheese. Serve with plenty of French or Italian bread and red wine.

Serves eight.

POACHED STUFFED CHICKEN BREASTS
  3 *whole chicken breasts, boned, skinned, and cut in half*
  6 *tablespoons butter*
  3 *tablespoons chopped shallots or onion*
  4 *tablespoons chopped parsley*
  1 *teaspoon dried thyme or 1½ teaspoons dried tarragon*
  1½ *teaspoons salt*
  Chicken broth

For the Sauce
  3 *tablespoons butter*
  3 *tablespoons flour*
  1 *cup cream*
  2 *egg yolks, lightly beaten*
  1 *teaspoon lemon juice*
  Chopped parsley

❧ Open the fold in each half-breast and flatten between pieces of waxed paper to make uniform in thickness. Mix the butter with the shallots, herbs, and salt. Spread the mixture over one side of each breast, then fold in half and secure with small skewers or tooth-picks. Arrange the six pieces in a large skillet and cover with chicken broth. Bring to a simmer over medium heat and cook for 12 minutes, or until the breasts are just done, turning once. Transfer to a warm ovenproof dish. Reduce the poaching liquid over high heat for a few minutes, then strain and set aside.

Melt the butter for the sauce in a heavy saucepan, stir in the flour, and cook over medium heat for a minute or so. Stir in 1½ cups of the poaching liquid and continue to stir over low heat until thickened. Blend the cream and egg yolks together, add a little of the hot sauce to temper the mixture, then stir all of it back into the sauce. Add the lemon juice, and taste for seasoning. Continue to cook until thickened, but do not allow to come to a boil.

Spoon the sauce over the chicken breasts, and place under a broiler briefly to glaze. Garnish with chopped parsley.

Serves four to six.

DJAJ M'KALLI

This is an interesting poached chicken dish from North Africa.

2 chickens, 3 pounds each, cut into serving pieces
2 tablespoons coarse salt
6 cloves garlic
1 cup vegetable oil
2 teaspoons ground ginger
1 teaspoon turmeric
1 teaspoon black pepper
Good pinch of saffron
3 large onions, grated
4 tablespoons butter
2 cups water
2 cups chicken stock
1 cup soft ripe olives
A few slices of pickled lemon (see page 45)

～ Start this chicken dish the day before. Wash and drain the chicken pieces and remove all fat, then rub well with a mixture of coarse salt and 3 of the garlic cloves chopped. Let stand 1 hour; wipe off. Rub with a mixture of vegetable oil, ginger, turmeric, black pepper, and saffron. Put in a large bowl with any remaining oil mixture; cover and refrigerate overnight.

Next day, put the chicken in a very large pot with the onions, butter, the 3 remaining cloves of garlic (finely chopped), water, and chicken stock. Bring to a boil, reduce the heat, cover, and simmer until the chicken is tender, 40 to 45 minutes. Remove the chicken and rapidly boil the broth down to a thick, rich sauce, stirring often. Correct seasoning. Add the soft ripe olives and a few slices of pickled lemon. Return the chicken to the simmering sauce to reheat. Serve with saffron rice.

Serves ten to twelve.

Pickled Lemons

8 large lemons
½ cup coarse salt
Olive oil or half olive oil and half peanut oil

～ Slice the lemons ½ inch thick, and place in a colander. Cover with salt, and wrap the colander with plastic wrap. Let stand for 24 hours. Remove the wrap, rinse the lemon well, and arrange in fruit jars or other jars with covers. Add enough oil to completely cover the slices. Cover and let stand for 1 to 2 weeks before using.

Pickled lemons will keep indefinitely if kept covered with oil. If additional salt is needed after the slices have ripened, add 1 tablespoon of salt to each jar.

CREOLE CHICKEN

This recipe, while not strictly a poached chicken, seems to belong here rather than with the casserole dishes. It is a hearty, flavorful dish, suitable for a large family or for a buffet. Choose a bird that can take long, slow cooking.

1 large poaching fowl, 5 to 6 pounds, cut up
Flour for dredging
6 tablespoons clarified butter
4 large onions, finely chopped
1 stalk celery, finely chopped
⅔ cup chopped parsley
3 green peppers, seeded and finely chopped
5 cloves garlic, chopped
1½ cups tomato purée
½ teaspoon crushed rosemary leaves
1 tablespoon paprika
¼ teaspoon cayenne
2 teaspoons salt
1 teaspoon freshly ground black pepper
1 tablespoon sweet chili powder
1 bay leaf, crushed
Boiling water or stock to cover

 Dredge the chicken pieces in flour and brown quickly in the butter in a large skillet. Transfer the chicken to a deep kettle, leaving the butter in the skillet. Add the chopped onions, celery, parsley, green peppers, and garlic and sauté until the onions soften. Beforehand, these vegetables may be put through a coarse chopper or food processor if you wish. Scoop out in spoonfuls and place on the chicken in the kettle. Add a little hot water to the skillet, rinse well and add to the kettle. Add the tomato purée seasoned with the rosemary, paprika, cayenne, salt, black pepper, sweet chili powder, and crushed bay leaf.

Add enough boiling water or stock to cover the chicken and stir briskly over a hot fire till the liquid boils. Reduce the heat and simmer slowly until the chicken is very tender, and the sauce reaches a velvety smoothness (see variation). Cooking time varies from 3 to 4 hours. Serve with boiled rice or spoon bread.

Serves eight for a buffet supper dish or six for a dinner.

Variation
If you wish, remove the chicken and thicken the sauce with a roux made with ¾ cup flour and 8 tablespoons butter.

Broiled Chicken

Broiling chickens weigh from 1½ to 3 pounds and are usually served split in half or quartered, depending on size. It is best to remove the necks and backbones and flatten slightly before broiling. Be sure to preheat the broiler and rub the broiler pan rack with butter or oil.

BASIC BROILED CHICKEN

Brush the chicken halves or quarters well with butter or oil. Place on a greased rack, skin side down, and broil about 4 inches from moderate heat for 12 to 14 minutes, depending on the size of the chicken. Brush with butter if it seems too dry. Season with salt and pepper, turn skin side up, and brush again with butter. Continue to broil gently, basting once or twice, for another 12 to 14 minutes. Test for tenderness with a fork; or pierce the thigh joint with a thin, sharp knife. If the juices run slightly pink (my preference) or clear, the chicken is done.

BROILED CHICKEN WITH ROSEMARY BUTTER

2 teaspoons chopped fresh rosemary or 1 teaspoon dried, crushed
1 tablespoon finely chopped parsley
1 tablespoon finely minced chives
Salt and freshly ground black pepper
1½ teaspoons lemon juice
4 tablespoons softened butter
1 broiler, split
¼ cup bread crumbs, toasted

Preheat the broiler. Blend the herbs, seasoning, lemon juice, and butter. Rub the chicken well with one-half the blended butter.

Place skin side down on a greased broiler rack and broil, 4 inches from moderate heat, for 12 to 14 minutes. Turn, brush with more butter, and broil, skin side up, for another 12 to 14 minutes. Sprinkle with the bread crumbs a minute or 2 before it is done. Serve with the remaining butter.

Serves two.

LEONIE DE SOUNIN'S HERBED BROILERS
This recipe is from Leonie de Sounin's book *Magic with Herbs*.

2 small broilers or fryers, about 1½ pounds each, left whole
½ lemon
2 tablespoons chopped parsley
1 teaspoon chopped, fresh rosemary or ½ teaspoon dried, crushed
1 tablespoon chopped chives
Pinch of ground ginger
6 tablespoons softened butter
Salt to taste
4 strips bacon

❧ Preheat the broiler.

Rub the chickens inside and out with half a lemon. Thoroughly blend the herbs and ginger with the butter and a bit of salt. Spread the herbed butter under the breast and thigh skin of the chickens. This will keep the meat juicy and impart an unbelievably good flavor to the bird as it cooks. Arrange the birds on their sides on a greased rack in a broiling pan and cover each with 2 strips of bacon. Broil under moderate heat for 5 minutes 4 inches from the heating unit. Turn, rearrange the bacon strips, and broil for another 5 minutes. Discard the bacon. Then place in the oven and roast at 400°F until brown and tender, about 15 to 20 minutes. Split in half and serve.

Serves four.

Variation

Combine 1 cup olive oil or vegetable oil, the juice of a lemon, 1 tablespoon chopped fresh tarragon or 1½ teaspoons dried, 2 tablespoons chopped parsley, 1 tablespoon chopped chives, a pinch of dried thyme, salt and freshly ground black pepper. Pour over the chicken in a bowl, and let marinate for at least 12 hours, turning several times. Remove the chickens from the marinade, dry with paper towels, and arrange on their sides on a rack in a broiling pan. Broil as directed above.

CHICKEN TERIYAKI

2 broilers, split
½ cup olive or peanut oil
⅔ cup Japanese soy sauce
2 tablespoons grated fresh ginger or 1 tablespoon chopped candied ginger, washed free of all sugar
2 cloves garlic, finely chopped
1 tablespoon grated tangerine or orange rind
¼ cup sherry

🐦 Place the chicken in a shallow pan. Blend all the remaining ingredients well and pour over the chicken. Turn the halves several times while they marinate, anywhere from an hour to 24 hours.

Preheat the broiler. Place the chicken a little farther from the heating unit than usual—at least 6 to 9 inches—to prevent the soy sauce from caramelizing. Broil bone side up, for 12 to 14 minutes, brushing once or twice with the marinade. Then turn carefully, brush again with marinade, and broil for another 12 to 14 minutes while continuing to baste.

Serves four.

DEVILED BROILERS

Broil chickens as directed in basic recipe, page 48. Just before they are ready to be served, remove from the broiler and sprinkle the skin side with hot buttered bread crumbs. Place in a hot oven for a few minutes to crisp the crumbs. Serve with the following sauce (enough for 4 to 6 servings):

1 onion, finely chopped
2 cloves garlic, finely chopped
6 tablespoons butter or bacon fat
1 cup tomato sauce
2 tablespoons Worcestershire sauce
½ teaspoon dry mustard
Giblets from the chickens, chopped and poached until tender
Salt and freshly ground black pepper to taste
Chopped parsley

In a skillet, sauté the onion and garlic in the butter or bacon fat. When transparent, add the tomato sauce, Worcestershire sauce, dry mustard, chopped giblets, and salt and pepper. Blend thoroughly and allow to simmer for 5 minutes. At the last minute stir in the degreased juices from the broiling pan. Add chopped parsley and serve with the crusty broilers.

DEVILED SQUAB CHICKEN WITH SAUCE BÉARNAISE

6 squab chickens, about 1 to 1½ pounds each, split

½ cup soy sauce

½ cup sherry

2 tablespoons Dijon mustard

1 tablespoon Tabasco

½ cup olive oil

1 cup melted butter, or as needed

3 cups bread crumbs, toasted, or as needed

1½ teaspoons freshly ground black pepper

Fresh watercress for garnish

Sauce béarnaise (see page 239)

Marinate the chickens for 2 hours, turning often, in a mixture of the soy sauce, sherry, mustard, Tabasco, and oil. Preheat the broiler. Broil, skin side down for 6 to 8 minutes, then turn and broil another 6 minutes. Remove from the broiler, dip in melted butter, and roll in the bread crumbs mixed with the pepper. Return to the broiler for 2 minutes; watch carefully. Turn, brush with butter, and broil another 2 minutes. Garnish with fresh watercress and serve with the sauce béarnaise.

Serves six.

STUFFED BROILED CHICKEN BREASTS

2 whole chicken breasts, split
4 tablespoons butter
¼ cup chopped parsley
¼ cup chopped chives or green onions
1 teaspoon dried basil
Heavy cream
Salt and freshly ground black pepper

Preheat the broiler.

Using a thin-bladed sharp knife, make a small pocket in each of the breasts. Cream the butter with the parsley, chives or green onions, and basil. Stuff the chicken breasts with this mixture and secure the opening with a toothpick. Brush the breasts with additional butter and broil under moderate heat for 10 to 12 minutes, turning once, starting bone side up. Just before they are finished, brush them with heavy cream and sprinkle with salt and pepper. Serve with tiny new potatoes dressed with crumbled bacon.

Serves four.

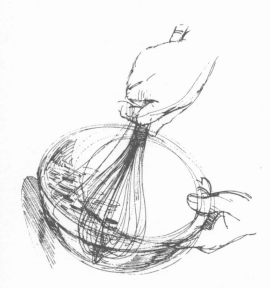

BARBECUE CHICKEN

3 to 4 broilers, split

2 medium onions, chopped

¼ cup olive oil

1 cup Italian tomato purée

1 teaspoon salt

1 teaspoon dried basil

½ cup honey

½ cup rich broth or stock

¼ cup Worcestershire sauce

1 teaspoon dry mustard

½ cup dry red wine

Sauté the onions in the olive oil until soft. Add all the rest of the ingredients except the chicken and wine and simmer gently for 10 to 15 minutes. Add the wine and heat through. Cool. Marinate the chicken halves in this mixture for 2 to 3 hours, turning them frequently to be sure they are well bathed.

Meanwhile prepare a charcoal fire. Place the chicken halves on a rack 3 to 4 inches from the coals and charcoal broil. Arrange bone side down and broil for 12 to 15 minutes. Brush with sauce, turn, and broil for another 12 to 15 minutes. Test for doneness by puncturing the thigh joint with a fork. When the juice runs clear or slightly pink, not red, the chicken is cooked. Do not overcook, or it will be dry and tasteless.

Serves six to eight.

Roast Chicken

Many of us remember the days when stuffed roasted chicken was the *pièce de résistance* of every Sunday's midday dinner, and we spent uncomfortable afternoons after eating too much of it. Nowadays it is everyday fare, but a roasted chicken still makes an elegant dish if it is perfectly cooked. I like to turn mine as it roasts to help keep the juices circulated and the skin evenly browned. It can be roasted either with or without stuffing. In either case it should be trussed.

Roasting chickens weigh anywhere fom 4 to 6 pounds, although the larger ones are hard to find. A bird of 4 to 5 pounds will be ample for four people. It should take 1 to 1¼ hours to cook. Wipe the chicken with a damp cloth and rub the cavity with half a lemon. If not stuffing, place a chunk—2 tablespoons—of butter inside and sprinkle with salt. Truss (see page 57). (If stuffing, fill the chicken lightly and close the vent with a skewer or seal with a piece of folded foil; proceed to truss.) Rub the skin generously with softened butter. Place on its side on a rack in a roasting pan. Roast for 20 minutes at 425°F. Turn on its other side, brush with melted butter, and roast for another 20 minutes. Then turn breast side up, brush with the pan juices, and salt and pepper well. Roast for a final 20 minutes. Prick the thigh joint to see if the juices run clear—don't be afraid of a little pinkness. Return to the oven, if necessary. If done, transfer to a hot platter or a carving board, and allow to settle for about 10 minutes before carving or cutting into quarters.

Variations

1. *With bacon:* Instead of buttering the chicken, drape it with strips of bacon, moving them to the top each time you turn the bird. Baste the skin with a combination of butter and bacon drippings.

2. *With herbed butter:* To 4 tablespoons of softened butter add the herb of your choice—1 tablespoon parsley, 1 tablespoon chives, 2 teaspoons fresh tarragon (or ½ teaspoon dried), or a combination of herbs. Blend well and spread under the loosened skin of the breast and thighs. Also put a tablespoon or so in the cavity if it is not stuffed.

STUFFING I

6 tablespoons butter, more if needed
1 onion, chopped
½ cup chopped celery
¼ cup chopped parsley
1 teaspoon dried thyme
Salt and freshly ground black pepper
2½ cups fine fresh bread crumbs

❧ Melt the butter in a skillet, add the onion and sauté until just soft. Add the rest of the ingredients and toss. If too dry, add more melted butter.

STUFFING II

Use a tarragon-flavored bread stuffing in the body cavity (see page 229). Reduce the quantity according to the size of your bird. Use well-flavored sausage meat to stuff the neck cavity. This two-stuffing arrangement would work best with an especially large roasting chicken.

TRUSSING

Trussing the chicken or game bird is the process of tying it and skewering it before placing it in the oven. It tends to keep the bird in a compact shape during the process of cooking. Fold the wings back so the tips are under the back. Press the legs and thighs close to the body and secure with a skewer or two run into the body of the bird. Tie string around the ends of the legs and around the tail and leave two equally long pieces of string. Carry the string around the wings, cross it in the middle of the back, and tie it securely over the breast. Always remove all string and skewers before carving and serving.

GIBLET SAUCE FOR ROAST CHICKEN

3 tablespoons fat from the roasting pan

3 tablespoons flour

1½ cups hot chicken broth (made from the giblets and neck) or milk, or
   as needed

Giblets, cooked and chopped

Salt and freshly ground black pepper to taste

🐚 Pour off all but 3 tablespoons fat from the roasting pan. Place the pan over low heat, add the flour and blend. Cook for 2 or 3 minutes. Add the heated broth or milk, scrape in all the brown residue in the pan, and stir until thickened. If too thick add a little more broth or milk. Add the chopped giblets, season to taste, and let cook for a few minutes more.

Variation

Tarragon Sauce: Make the sauce with fat, flour, and 1 cup of chicken or veal broth, as directed above. Add 1 tablespoon chopped fresh tarragon or 1 teaspoon dried tarragon. Then stir in ¾ cup heavy cream over low heat until smooth. Season to taste, and stir in 1 tablespoon chopped parsley.

DIET ROAST CHICKEN

2 broilers, about 2 to 2½ pounds each, split, with backbones removed

¼ pound fresh mushrooms, finely chopped

2 tablespoons softened unsalted margarine

6 finely chopped shallots

1 tablespoon finely chopped parsley

1 tablespoon chopped fresh rosemary or 1 teaspoon crushed dried

1 teaspoon dry mustard in ¼ cup water

🍃 Loosen the skin of the chickens by running a finger under it, being careful not to pierce the skin. Mix the rest of the ingredients, and spread about ¼ cup of the mixture under the skin of each chicken half. Arrange, skin side up, on a rack in a roasting pan, and bake at 400°F for 50 to 60 minutes, until nicely brown and done through.

Serves four.

ROAST CHICKEN SESAME

3 pounds chicken parts
Flour for dredging
1 egg, beaten with a little water
1 cup sesame seeds
6 tablespoons butter
¼ cup Cognac, warmed
½ cup dry white wine
4 tablespoons melted butter
½ cup heavy cream

❧ Dredge the chicken pieces well in flour, dip in beaten egg, and roll in sesame seeds till completely covered. Brown quickly in the 6 tablespoons of butter. Transfer the pieces to a large flameproof casserole, pour the Cognac over, and flambé.

Roast, uncovered, in a 325°F oven for 30 to 45 minutes, basting occasionally with a mixture of wine and melted butter. Remove from the oven. Add the cream to the pan, blend with the pan juices, and baste the chicken well. Return to the oven and cook for 20 minutes more.

Serve with crisp fried potatoes and a cucumber, onion, and tomato salad.

Serves four to six.

ROAST SQUAB CHICKEN WITH CURRIED RICE

This may also be prepared with fresh Cornish game hens.

1 heaping cup raw rice, washed
1 large onion, finely chopped
6 tablespoons butter
1 to 3 teaspoons good-quality curry powder, to taste
Dash of cayenne
Celery seeds
Chopped parsley
Salt and freshly ground pepper
1 teaspoon sugar
4 squab chickens, about 1 to 1½ pounds each
½ cup light cream

Cook the rice in salted water until just tender. Set aside. Sauté the onion in butter. When soft, stir in curry powder to taste. Add a dash of cayenne, a few celery seeds, chopped parsley, salt and pepper to taste, and the sugar. Combine with the rice.

Stuff each chicken with the curried rice; truss securely (see page 57). Place in a buttered baking dish and brown in a hot oven (425°F). Reduce the heat to 300°F, pour cream over the chickens, and bake until quite tender, about 45 minutes.

Serves two to four.

STUFFED SQUAB CHICKEN

3 cups finely chopped green onions

8 tablespoons butter

1½ pounds pork sausage meat

4 cups fresh bread crumbs

2 eggs, lightly beaten

½ cup finely chopped parsley

1 tablespoon fresh tarragon or 1½ teaspoons dried

½ cup plus ⅓ cup Cognac

Salt and freshly ground black pepper

6 squab chickens, about 1 pound each

Parsley sprigs or watercress for garnish

Sauté the green onions in 4 tablespoons of butter until limp, and then remove to a bowl. Set the rest of the butter aside, and allow to soften. Sauté the sausage meat in the same pan, separating it into small bits with a fork or wooden spoon, until it has cooked through and lost its raw look. Do not brown. In a large bowl combine the green onions, sausage meat, bread crumbs, eggs, parsley, tarragon, and ½ cup Cognac. Taste for seasoning, and add salt and pepper if necessary.

Stuff the chickens with this mixture, truss them (page 57), and spread the softened butter over the skin. Arrange on their sides on a rack in a baking pan. Roast at 400°F for 15 minutes, then turn on the other side and roast for another 15 minutes. Place chickens breast side up, baste with the pan juices, and continue to roast until nicely brown, about 10 minutes more.

Transfer to a hot platter. Degrease the juices in the pan, stir in the remaining ⅓ cup Cognac, and heat through, scraping up any residue at the bottom of the pan. Strain and pour over the chicken. Garnish the platter with sprigs of parsley or watercress.

Serves six.

STUFFED CHICKEN LEGS

6 large chicken legs
½ cup finely chopped onions
1 teaspoon finely chopped garlic
2 tablespoons butter
1 cup fresh bread crumbs
¼ cup finely chopped parsley
1 teaspoon dried thyme
1 teaspoon salt
½ teaspoon freshly ground black pepper
½ cup finely chopped pecans
¼ cup sherry
Flour
4 tablespoons melted butter

Optional Cream Sauce

3 tablespoons flour
1 cup heavy cream
Salt and freshly ground black pepper

✥ Using a small boning knife, split the flesh on the inside of each thigh to the joint and loosen the flesh from the bone. Cut around the joint—being careful not to pierce the skin—and push the flesh of the leg halfway down the bone, then sever the bone with poultry shears. This will leave the thigh and half of the leg boned for stuffing.

In a skillet sauté the onions and garlic in the butter over medium heat until the onions are translucent. Add the bread crumbs, herbs, seasonings, and nuts, and combine well. Blend in the sherry. Stuff the legs, and secure the flesh with small skewers or toothpicks. Dust with flour and place, seam side down, in a buttered baking dish or pan. Brush with melted butter. Bake in a 400°F oven for 40 minutes.

To serve with a cream sauce: Degrease the pan juices and combine with the flour in a small, heavy saucepan. Add the residue from the baking dish, loosening it with a little hot water if necessary. Over medium heat gradually stir in the cream and continue to stir until thickened. Season with salt and pepper to taste.

Serves six.

Braised Chicken, Fricassees, Casseroles

BRAISED STUFFED CHICKEN

8 ounces noodles
8 tablespoons butter, approximately
¼ pound chicken livers, chopped
¼ pound mushrooms, chopped
½ teaspoon freshly grated nutmeg
½ cup freshly grated Parmesan cheese
½ cup heavy cream
1 tablespoon chopped parsley
Salt and freshly ground black pepper to taste
1 roasting chicken, 4 pounds
1 cup chicken broth

Cook the noodles in boiling salted water just until tender. Drain and toss with a bit of butter to keep from sticking together.

Sauté the chopped livers and mushrooms in 2 tablespoons butter over low heat for 3 minutes. Add to the noodles, along with the nutmeg, grated cheese, cream, parsley, and salt and pepper, and blend well. Gently stuff the chicken, sew up the vent, and truss (see page 57). If there is any extra stuffing, place it in a small baking dish, dot with butter, and cook with the chicken for 10 to 15 minutes.

Preheat the oven to 350°F.

Heat the remaining butter in an ovenproof casserole and brown the chicken quickly, turning on all sides in the casserole to achieve an evenness of color. Add the chicken broth and cover the casserole. Place in the preheated oven and cook for 1½ hours, basting every 20 minutes with a little broth. Serve with the degreased pan juices; or if you prefer a thickened sauce, melt 2 tablespoons butter in a saucepan and stir in 2 tablespoons flour. Allow to cook for a moment, then add the degreased pan juices and ½ cup milk. Stir over a medium flame till the sauce thickens, adding more milk if necessary. Season with salt and pepper to taste.

Serves four to six.

BRAISED LEMON CHICKEN

1 roasting chicken, 4 pounds
2½ lemons
2 tablespoons olive oil
1 large onion, finely chopped
2 teaspoons turmeric
2 cups chicken broth or water
2 cans (1 pound) chick-peas or garbanzos, drained
4 cloves garlic, crushed
Salt and freshly ground black pepper

Rub the chicken inside and out with half a lemon. Heat the oil in a deep braising pan or Dutch oven. Sauté the onion in the oil until soft and golden. Sprinkle with half the turmeric and mix well. Rub the chicken with the remaining turmeric.

Sear the chicken in the oil with the onion, turning it so that it colors a rather deep yellow on all sides. Add the broth or water, the drained chick-peas, juice of 2 lemons, garlic, and salt and pepper to taste. Bring to a boil, then reduce the heat and simmer, covered, for 1 hour or longer, or until the chicken is just tender. Remove the chicken from the sauce, cut in serving pieces, and serve with the chick-peas and the sauce.

Serves four to six.

HUNGARIAN CHICKEN

6 chicken legs with thighs

1 cup flour, or as needed

2 tablespoons paprika

2 teaspoons salt

½ teaspoon freshly ground black pepper

4 tablespoons butter, or as needed

¼ cup cooking oil, or as needed

1½ cups chopped onion

1 cup broth, or as needed

1 cup sour cream

1 tablespoon finely cut lemon zest

Put the chicken pieces in a bag with the flour, 1 tablespoon paprika, and salt and pepper; shake well. Heat the butter and oil in a heavy skillet till quite hot, and brown the chicken pieces on both sides. Transfer to a piece of foil or paper towels. Add the onion to the skillet and brown very well, using additional butter and oil if needed. Return the chicken pieces to the pan with the broth and remaining paprika and simmer, covered, till the chicken is just tender, about 20 minutes. If the broth is absorbed, add more. Transfer the chicken to a hot serving dish. Add the sour cream to the pan off heat and stir into the pan juices; heat for 1 minute but do not boil. Pour over the chicken pieces. Sprinkle the lemon zest on top.

Serve with grilled tomatoes and with noodles tossed with butter and crisp croutons.

Serves four to six.

COUNTRY CAPTAIN

Based on an East Indian curry, this dish owes its name to the term for a native Indian captain in the pay of his English colonizers. The version given here comes from Cecily Brownstone, the Associated Press food columnist.

1 fryer, about 2¼ pounds
¼ cup flour
1 teaspoon salt
¼ teaspoon freshly ground black pepper
4 tablespoons butter
⅓ cup finely diced onion
⅓ cup finely diced green pepper
1 clove garlic, crushed
1½ teaspoons curry powder
½ teaspoon dried thyme, crushed
1 can (1 pound) stewed tomatoes
3 tablespoons dried currants, washed and drained
Blanched toasted almonds

The chicken should be cut to yield 2 pieces of breast, 2 wings, 2 legs, and 2 second joints. Save the back, wing tips, neck, and giblets for a broth. Dredge the chicken with a mixture of the flour, salt, and pepper. Heat the butter in a large skillet and brown the chicken. Transfer to a hot platter. Add the onion, green pepper, garlic, curry powder, and thyme to the skillet. Stir over low heat and scrape loose the browned residue in the pan. Add the stewed tomatoes, with their liquid. Arrange the chicken in the skillet, skin side up. Cover and cook slowly until tender, about 20 to 30 minutes. Stir the currants into the sauce. Serve topped with the toasted almonds.

Serves two to three.

Variation
For the final cooking, the dish may be baked, covered, in a 325°F oven until tender, about 45 minutes.

CURRIED CHICKEN

2 frying chickens, about 3 pounds each, cut into 8 pieces
2½ cups salted water or 2 cups chicken broth
1 eggplant, peeled and diced
3 tablespoons olive oil
½ cup water
2 apples (unpeeled), chopped
2 medium onions, chopped
10 tablespoons butter
2 tablespoons curry powder
Pinch of cayenne
1 teaspoon chopped garlic
½ teaspoon ground ginger
2 tablespoons chutney
2 tablespoons tomato purée
Salt

Make a broth with the necks, giblets, and wing tips of the chickens, using salted water or chicken broth. Sauté the eggplant in the olive oil over medium heat for about 5 minutes, then add water, cover, and simmer gently until soft. Separately sauté the apples and onions in 4 tablespoons of butter until soft, then add the curry powder, cayenne, garlic, ginger, and 1 cup of the chicken broth. Cover and simmer for 30 minutes. Then add the chutney, tomato purée, eggplant, and a second cup of broth, and simmer for another 30 minutes.

Sauté the chicken pieces in the remaining butter until nicely browned on all sides, and sprinkle with salt. Taste the curry sauce for seasoning, adding salt if necessary, and dilute with a little water or broth if it is too thick. Add the chicken and simmer for about 10 minutes, or until cooked through and well flavored with the sauce.

Serve with chutney, chopped unsalted peanuts or slivered almonds, grated coconut, chopped hard-boiled egg, and raisins soaked in Cognac.

Serves six to eight.

COQ AU VIN

6 tablespoons butter

1 fryer, 3 pounds, quartered

1 teaspoon salt

½ teaspoon freshly ground black pepper

¼ cup Cognac

1 bottle dry red wine, as needed

Bouquet garni (1 sprig thyme, 1 bay leaf, 1 sprig parsley,
*   6 peppercorns, tied in cheese-cloth)*

12 small white onions

3 slices salt pork, cut in ½ pieces

12 mushroom caps, quartered

Beurre manié (3 tablespoons flour and 3 tablespoons butter
*   kneaded together)*

❧ Melt 3 tablespoons butter in a large, heavy skillet and brown the chicken over medium-high heat, about 5 minutes on each side. Sprinkle with salt and pepper. Drain off the butter, pour the Cognac over the chicken, and flambé. Add enough wine to just cover the chicken, then add the bouquet garni. Cover the pan and simmer for 30 minutes, or until tender. Test the pieces of white meat first, and if done, transfer to a warm platter while the dark meat continues to cook. Remove the bouquet garni.

Meanwhile, melt the remaining butter in another skillet and brown the onions and salt pork. Then cover and cook very slowly for about 20 minutes, or until the onions are tender. Add the mushrooms and cook for another 4 minutes.

When the chicken has been removed from the pan, degrease the sauce and bring to a boil. Add the beurre manié a bit at a time until the sauce has thickened slightly. Correct the seasoning. Add the onions, salt pork, and mushrooms to the chicken, and pour the sauce over all.

Serves four.

BROWN FRICASSEE OF CHICKEN

1 roasting chicken, 4 to 5 pounds, cut up
Flour
Salt and freshly ground black pepper
4 tablespoons butter
1 medium onion, finely chopped
1 garlic clove, finely chopped
Pinch each of dried thyme and marjoram
Boiling chicken broth or water to cover
¾ cup heavy cream

Dredge chicken pieces with flour, salt, and pepper. Heat the butter in a heavy kettle and brown the onion and garlic. Add the chicken pieces and brown them nicely on all sides. Add the thyme and marjoram. Cover with boiling broth or water and simmer, covered, until tender, about 45 minutes. Add the cream and let it cook down for a few minutes. Correct the seasoning and serve with boiled rice. If you wish a thicker sauce, you may thicken it with beurre manié—small balls of flour and butter blended well.

Serves four to six.

AMERICAN FRICASSEE OF CHICKEN

1 roasting chicken, 4 pounds, cut up, neck and giblets reserved
1 small veal knuckle
Salt to taste
1 onion
1 sprig parsley
1 sprig fresh thyme
6 cups water
1 bay leaf
2 cloves
3 tablespoons butter
3 tablespoons flour
¾ cup heavy cream
Freshly ground black pepper to taste
Pinch of freshly grated nutmeg
Chopped parsley

Combine the neck, wing tips, giblets, veal knuckle, salt, onion, and parsley and thyme sprigs with the water. Simmer for 1 hour. Strain the broth.

Pour the boiling broth over the pieces of chicken in a large kettle. Add the bay leaf and cloves and simmer with the cover on the kettle till the chicken is tender. This should take about 45 minutes. In a heavy skillet, melt the butter and add the flour. Blend well, then add 2 cups of the chicken broth and stir until it begins to thicken. Gradually add the cream, stirring constantly till the mixture is thoroughly blended. Season with salt, pepper, and a pinch of nutmeg. Arrange the pieces of chicken on a hot platter, surround with boiled rice or buttered noodles, and pour the sauce over all. Sprinkle with a little chopped parsley.

Serves four to six.

BLANQUETTE OF CHICKEN

1 roasting chicken, 4 to 5 pounds, cut up
Boiling chicken broth or water to cover
1 onion, peeled
1 carrot
1 stalk celery
Bouquet garni (parsley, chervil, and marjoram tied in cheesecloth)
Salt and freshly ground black pepper
2 tablespoons butter
2 tablespoons flour
1 cup cream, mixed with 2 egg yolks
Lemon juice to taste

Place chicken pieces in a kettle and cover with boiling broth or water. Add the onion, carrot, celery, and bouquet garni. Let simmer until tender, about 1 hour. Add salt and pepper to taste.

When the chicken is tender, remove it to a hot platter or casserole. Make a roux by blending the butter with the flour in a skillet; cook gently, taking care not to brown it. Strain the broth, add to it the roux, and stir till it has thickened. Add the cream blended with the egg yolks and stir constantly till well combined with the sauce. Add a few drops of lemon juice, correct the seasoning, and pour over the chicken. Serve with sautéed mushrooms and boiled rice.

Serves four to six.

FRICASSEE OF CHICKEN WITH WHITE WINE

1 roasting chicken, 4 pounds, cut up
½ lemon
4 tablespoons butter
1 pound tiny white onions, peeled
½ pound sliced mushrooms
Dry white wine to cover
3 or 4 leaves fresh tarragon
Salt and freshly ground black pepper
¾ cup cream

Rub each chicken piece with the lemon half and allow to sit for 15 minutes. Gently sauté the chicken pieces in the butter in a deep skillet or casserole till they are a pale golden shade. Add the onions and sliced mushrooms. Pour in enough wine to cover and add the fresh tarragon. Cover and simmer very gently for 45 minutes, or until the chicken is tender. Season with salt and pepper to taste, and just before serving blend the cream well into the sauce. Serve with boiled rice.

Serves four to six.

PAELLA

For a variation of the Spanish paella, try making it with chicken wings rather than the cut-up whole chicken.

> *12 chicken wings*
> *Flour*
> *6 tablespoons peanut oil*
> *Salt and freshly ground black pepper to taste*
> *1 onion, finely chopped*
> *2 garlic cloves, chopped*
> *1½ cups raw rice*
> *Boiling chicken broth or water to cover*
> *Pinch of saffron*
> *1 or 2 Italian or Spanish sausages, sliced*
> *½ cup chopped canned tomatoes*
> *24 clams, in their shells*
> *12 shrimp, in their shells*
> *3 pimientos, cut in thin strips*
> *½ package (10 ounces) frozen green peas, thawed*

≈ Flour the chicken wings, and brown in oil in a large skillet or paella pan. Season with salt and pepper, remove to a platter, and keep warm.

Sauté the onion and garlic in the oil until soft. Add the rice and stir until well coated with oil and translucent. Pour over it enough boiling chicken broth or water to cover, then season with salt, pepper, and saffron and let the liquid cook down. Add the chicken wings, sliced sausages, tomatoes, and additional liquid, if necessary. Simmer over low heat until the rice is just beginning to get tender; add the clams and shrimp. Cook until the shrimp are pink and cooked through and the clam shells open. Nearly all the liquid should have cooked away at this point; if it has not, raise the heat until it evaporates, leaving the rice firm and the grains separate. Garnish with pimiento strips and peas (the heat from the paella will warm them through).

Serves six.

CHICKEN CALANDRIA

This buffet dish comes from an old Mexican cook, Calandria, who made many pilgrimages to California to prepare and teach her national dishes. She would arrive complete with aprons, *metate*, and all the mysterious ingredients that go into Mexican foods.

1 roasting chicken, 5 pounds, cut up, or an equivalent amount of
* chicken breasts and legs*
½ cup white water-ground cornmeal
½ cup olive oil
3 medium white onions, finely chopped
3 cloves garlic, finely chopped
¾ cup dry red wine, heated
Pinch each of mace and dried marjoram
1 teaspoon sesame seeds
½ teaspoon caraway seeds
3 cups boiling water
Salt to taste
1 cup whole blanched almonds
1 cup pitted green olives
¼ cup sweet chili powder

Dredge the pieces of chicken in the cornmeal. Save any cornmeal left behind. Heat the olive oil in a large casserole. When hot but not smoking, sear the chicken slightly on all sides. Lower the heat, add the onions and garlic, and mix well with the chicken. Add the wine, mace, marjoram, sesame seeds, caraway seeds, boiling water, and salt. Cover and allow to simmer gently for 10 minutes.

Add the almonds, olives, and chili powder and simmer for another 20 to 30 minutes, stirring occasionally.

Mix a little of the reserved cornmeal with water and add to thicken the sauce to the desired consistency, stirring continuously to keep the cornmeal from forming lumps or sticking to the bottom of the pot.

Put aside until ready to serve, for this dish is much better reheated.

Serves five to six.

CHICKEN CASSEROLE WITH RICE

1 roasting chicken, 3 pounds, cut up
½ lemon
Flour for dredging
Salt and freshly ground black pepper
¼ pound bacon, cut in slivers
6 carrots, scraped and quartered
3 medium onions, sliced
1 large clove garlic, peeled
1 teaspoon dried tarragon
½ cup chopped parsley
1½ cups raw rice
Chicken broth as needed

❧ Preheat the oven to 375°F.

Rub chicken pieces with half a lemon, then dredge with flour, salt, and pepper. Fry the bacon slivers in a skillet till crisp. Remove the bacon and place in an ovenproof casserole. Brown the chicken in the bacon fat left in the skillet, a few pieces at a time so it achieves an even color. Place in the casserole, along with the carrots, sliced onions, garlic, tarragon, and parsley.

Brown the rice in the skillet, adding more fat if necessary. Add this to the casserole and pour in a strong, well-seasoned broth to cover. Bake, covered, in the preheated oven for 1 hour, or until the rice is thoroughly cooked and the liquid is entirely cooked away. If the broth cooks away before the rice is soft, add a little more to the casserole.

Serves four to six.

ITALIAN CASSEROLE OF CHICKEN

An old Italian cook taught me this dish. She had created it in an emergency, and it was so successful that she kept it in her repertoire and wove a beautiful story around it: "An old Tuscan dish handed down through generations," she said.

> 1 roasting chicken, 4 pounds
> Celery leaves
> 3 carrots
> 1 sprig parsley
> Salt and freshly ground black pepper
> Boiling water to cover
> ¼ pound bacon, cut in slivers
> 2 medium onions, finely chopped
> 2 cloves garlic, finely chopped
> ¼ teaspoon dried thyme
> ¼ cup olive oil
> ½ cup black Italian or Greek olives, pitted
> 1 green pepper, seeded and cut into julienne
> 2 tablespoons butter
> 6 large tomatoes, peeled and quartered
> 1 tablespoon chopped fresh basil or 1 teaspoon dried
> 1 pound spaghetti
> 3 tablespoons chopped parsley
> 3 eggs
> ⅔ cup freshly grated Parmesan cheese

Place the chicken in a kettle with some celery leaves, the carrots, parsley sprig, and 2 teaspoons salt. Cover with boiling water and simmer till tender, about 1 hour. Remove from the broth and allow to cool slightly. Strip all the meat from the bones, cutting the larger pieces into small chunks. Place in a large heatproof casserole.

Cook the bacon in a skillet over a low heat until crisp. Remove and add to the casserole. Sauté the onions, garlic, and thyme in the bacon fat till the onions are transparent but not browned. Add to the casserole.

Heat the olive oil in a clean skillet and sauté the olives and green pepper for 3 to 4 minutes. Add salt to taste and add to the casserole.

Finally, melt the butter in a skillet, add the tomatoes and basil, and cook till well blended but not mushy. Salt and pepper to taste and add to the casserole.

Preheat the oven to 400°F.

Cook the spaghetti in boiling salted water till *al dente*. This should take from 9 to 12 minutes. Drain and toss with all ingredients in the casserole. Add the chopped parsley.

Beat the eggs till lemon colored and add the grated cheese to make a thick paste. Spread carefully over the spaghetti mixture. Bake in the preheated oven till the eggs and cheese are set and browned. Serve with hot French or Italian bread, which has been split and spread with a mixture of butter, chopped chives, parsley, and a whiff of garlic; a large green salad; and plenty of good claret.

Serves eight to ten.

OLD-FASHIONED CHICKEN CASSEROLE

6 tablespoons butter or butter and oil

1 roasting chicken, 4 to 5 pounds, cut up

3 medium carrots, scraped and cut into julienne

1 stalk celery, trimmed and cut into julienne

12 small white onions, peeled

1 cup chicken broth

½ teaspoon thyme

Salt and freshly ground black pepper to taste

2 cups thick béchamel sauce (page 237)

Lemon juice to taste

1 package (10 ounces) frozen small peas

❧ Preheat the oven to 350°F.

Heat the butter or butter and oil in a skillet and brown the pieces of chicken quickly on all sides. Transfer to a 4-quart casserole with a cover.

Add the carrots, celery, onions, broth, thyme, and salt and pepper to the casserole. Cover, place in the preheated oven, and cook for about 30 minutes.

Prepare 2 cups of thick béchamel sauce. Pour over the chicken and vegetable mixture, cover it again, and continue cooking for 30 to 35 minutes, or until the chicken is tender.

Cook the peas according to directions on the package. Add to the casserole, and stir in the lemon juice just as you send it to the table.

Tiny new potatoes are perfect with this dish; or serve rice.

Serves six.

CASSEROLE OF CHICKEN WITH WHITE WINE

1 roasting chicken, 4 pounds

½ lemon

Stuffing of your choice (see pages 227-235)

5 tablespoons olive oil, butter, or bacon fat

1 cup white wine, or as needed

12 small white onions, peeled

15 small new potatoes, peeled

Salt and freshly ground black pepper

12 mushrooms, cleaned and halved or quartered, if large

1 sprig parsley

Preheat the oven to 325°F.

Rub the inside of the chicken with half a lemon. Stuff and truss the chicken (see page 57). Brown well in a skillet in olive oil, butter, or bacon fat. Place in a flameproof casserole with ½ cup white wine. Cover and bake in the preheated oven for 45 minutes.

In the meantime, sauté the onions and potatoes in the fat remaining in the pan in which you browned the chicken, until nicely browned and partially cooked. Season with salt and pepper to taste.

Remove the casserole from the oven and add the potatoes, onions, mushrooms, and parsley sprig. Salt and pepper the chicken and add remaining wine, then cover and replace in the oven. Cook for another 30 minutes, or until the chicken is tender. Serve with the degreased pan juices, slightly thickened if you like, and garnish with the onions, potatoes, and mushrooms.

Serves four to six.

CHICKEN CASSEROLE WITH LENTILS

2 cups lentils

1 onion, stuck with 2 cloves

1 bay leaf

1 teaspoon salt

1 roasting chicken, 4 pounds, cut up

Flour for dredging

Salt and freshly ground black pepper

5 tablespoons butter

Boiling water or broth, if needed

Prepare the lentils. Presoak unprocessed lentils for several hours, then drain and place in a kettle with water to cover, an onion stuck with 2 cloves, a bay leaf, and salt. Bring to a boil, reduce the heat, and simmer until tender. (Quick-cooking lentils require no soaking, and will cook in 25 to 30 minutes.)

Preheat the oven to 350°F.

Dredge the chicken with flour, salt, and pepper. Heat the butter in a heavy skillet and brown the chicken very quickly. Transfer to a casserole. Add the lentils and the broth in which they were cooked. If there is not enough liquid to cover, add boiling water or broth. Place in the preheated oven and cook slowly for 1¼ to 1½ hours, adding more liquid if necessary.

Serves six.

Variation

For a more distinctive flavor, add to the casserole 6 or 7 slices of *cotechino* or other highly flavored pork sausage, such as the hot Italian variety.

CHICKEN TETRAZZINI

3 cups diced, cooked chicken
2 cups sauce suprême (page 238)
⅓ cup dry sherry
2 tablespoons chopped pimiento (optional)
Salt and freshly ground black pepper
12 ounces spaghetti
Buttered bread crumbs
Freshly grated Parmesan cheese

🍂 Heat the diced chicken in the sauce suprême. When it is thoroughly blended and heated through, add the sherry and pimiento. Season to taste.

Preheat the oven to 425°F.

Cook spaghetti in boiling, salted water till it is as tender as you like it. Drain and place in a buttered casserole or baking dish. Cover with the chicken mixture, then sprinkle with buttered crumbs and grated Parmesan cheese and bake in the preheated oven until the top has lightly browned.

Serves six to eight.

BAKED MUSTARD CHICKEN

2 whole chicken breasts, boned, skinned, and cut in half
Flour
2 to 3 tablespoons butter
1 tablespoon olive oil
1 tablespoon mustard— Dijon, herbed, or to your taste
1 medium onion, finely chopped
½ cup finely chopped mushrooms
1 cup heavy cream
Salt and freshly ground black pepper
2 teaspoons lemon juice
2 tablespoons chopped parsley

Dust the chicken breasts with flour, and sauté in a heavy skillet in 2 tablespoons of the butter and the oil until delicately brown on both sides; they should not cook through. Transfer to a shallow baking dish, and spread each breast generously with mustard. Add the onion to the skillet, and remaining butter, if needed, and sauté over medium heat for 2 or 3 minutes. Add the mushrooms and cook for another 2 minutes. Blend in the heavy cream and heat through. Add salt and pepper to taste—start with ¼ teaspoon of salt; go easy on the pepper. Pour the mixture over the chicken, and bake in a 350°F oven for about 30 minutes, or until the chicken is tender to the fork. Taste the sauce for seasoning, and add the lemon juice. Garnish with the parsley. Serve with rice.

Serves four.

CHICKEN WITH FORTY CLOVES OF GARLIC

8 chicken legs with thighs
40 cloves garlic
4 stalks celery
⅔ cup olive oil
6 sprigs parsley
1 tablespoon chopped fresh tarragon or 1½ teaspoons dried
½ cup dry vermouth
2½ teaspoons salt
¼ teaspoon freshly ground black pepper
Pinch of freshly grated nutmeg

Preheat the oven to 375°F.

Wash the chicken legs and thighs and thoroughly dry. Peel the garlic, leaving the cloves whole. Trim the celery, then cut in thin slices. Put the oil in a shallow dish or a plate and turn the chicken in the oil to coat on all sides. Reserve the unused oil. Lay the celery slices in the bottom of a heavy casserole with a tight-fitting cover. Add the parsley and tarragon, then lay the chicken pieces on top. Pour the vermouth over the chicken, and add 1 teaspoon salt, the pepper, and nutmeg.

Pour the reserved oil into the casserole, then toss in all the garlic and sprinkle with the remaining salt. Put a piece of aluminum foil over the casserole and then cover to make a tight seal; or make a thick, heavy flour and water paste to seal the lid, and cover lid and paste with another layer of foil. Bake in the preheated oven for 1½ hours without removing the lid.

Serve with hot toast or thin slices of pumpernickel—to be spread with the garlic sauce. You will find that the garlic has been tamed in the cooking and acquired a delicious buttery quality.

Serves six to eight.

Creamed chicken

Creamed chicken has become a cliché in the American kitchen and is looked upon by sophisticated cooks with some condescension. However, it can be a pleasant dish, and even a dish of distinction, if the chicken is of good quality and the sauce is prepared with care.

CREAMED CHICKEN

1½ cups béchamel sauce (page 237)
2 tablespoons Madeira, sherry, Cognac, or bourbon
2 cups diced, cooked chicken
1 tablespoon chopped parsley
4 slices toast, muffins, or patty shells; or boiled rice

🌭 Prepare the béchamel sauce, and when thickened add the Madeira or other flavoring. Combine with diced chicken in the upper part of a double boiler. Place over simmering water, cover, and allow to heat for 8 to 10 minutes, or until the chicken is blended with sauce and thoroughly heated. Add the chopped parsley. Serve on toast or muffins, in patty shells, or on rice.

Serves four.

CREAMED CHICKEN AND MUSHROOMS

½ pound mushrooms, cleaned

1½ cups water

Salt and freshly ground black pepper

2 tablespoons butter

2 cups diced, cooked chicken

2 cups béchamel sauce (page 237)

2 egg yolks

Lemon juice to taste

❧ Remove the stems from the mushrooms and slice caps. Chop the stems and simmer in the water for 30 to 40 minutes. Drain off the broth, add salt to taste, and reserve. Discard the chopped stems. Lightly sauté the sliced mushrooms in the butter.

Heat the chicken in the béchamel sauce in a double boiler and add the sliced mushrooms and about half the broth. Mix well and remove from the heat. Allow to cool slightly before adding the egg yolks mixed with the remaining broth. Return to low heat and stir till well blended and smooth. Taste for seasoning and squeeze in a few drops of lemon juice.

Serves six.

CHICKEN À LA KING

In its day—the 1920s and 1930s—this dish was considered a classic.

3 cups diced, cooked chicken
3 tablespoons chopped pimiento or roasted peppers
3 cups sauce suprême (page 238)
6 tablespoons sherry
1 cup sliced mushrooms, sautéed in 4 tablespoons butter
1 tablespoon chopped green pepper
1 tablespoon grated onion
3 tablespoons chopped parsley
Salt and freshly ground black pepper to taste
Lemon juice to taste

❧ Heat the chicken and pimiento or roasted peppers in the sauce, and add the sherry. Add the sautéed mushrooms, green pepper, onion, parsley, and seasonings.

Serves six.

CREAMED CHICKEN IN NOODLE RING

8 ounces noodles
4 eggs, separated
1 cup milk or light cream
Salt and freshly ground black pepper to taste
Chicken à la king (see above)
Strips of pimiento or broiled mushroom caps for garnish

❧ Preheat the oven to 350°F.

Cook the noodles in boiling, salted water till *al dente*, about 9 minutes. Drain. Beat the egg yolks till lemon colored. Add the milk or light cream, salt, and pepper. Combine with the noodles. Beat the egg whites until very stiff and fold into the noodle mixture. Turn into a well-greased 6-cup ring mold. Place the mold in a pan of hot water and bake in the preheated oven for 50 to 60 minutes. Unmold on a platter. Fill with hot chicken à la king and garnish with strips of pimiento or broiled mushroom caps.

Serves six.

CREAMED CHICKEN WITH CLAMS

1½ cups diced, cooked chicken
2 cups velouté sauce (page 238), made with 1 cup clam broth
1 cup raw small whole clams or minced razor clams
3 tablespoons cream
Salt and freshly ground black pepper
1 tablespoon chopped parsley

❧ Heat the chicken and sauce in a double boiler. Add the clams and cook gently for a few minutes more or until the clams are heated through. Stir in the cream, taste for seasoning, and add the parsley.

Serves four.

Variation
With oysters: Proceed as above, substituting oyster liquor in the velouté sauce and 1 cup raw oysters in the chicken mixture. Heat till the edges of the oysters curl.

SWISS ENCHILADAS

This Mexican dish is mild in seasoning, delicious, and agreeable to almost everyone. It is called "Swiss" because of the cream, which is true of all such dishes in Mexico.

>*1 onion, chopped*
>*Cooking oil*
>*1 clove garlic, crushed*
>*2 cups tomato purée*
>*2 green chilies, chopped*
>*2 cups chopped, cooked chicken*
>*Salt*
>*1 dozen tortillas*
>*2 cups heavy cream*
>*1 cup concentrated chicken stock*
>*½ pound jack cheese, sliced or grated*
>*Garnish: sliced avocado, sliced hard-boiled eggs, or green or ripe olives*

Preheat the oven to 350°F.

Prepare the stuffing. Sauté the onion in 2 tablespoons oil until soft. Then add the garlic, tomato purée, chilies, and chicken. Add salt to taste and simmer for about 10 minutes. Briefly heat the tortillas, one at a time, in about 1 inch hot oil. Do not let them get crisp, as they are to be rolled.

Heat the cream, and add the chicken stock. Dip each tortilla into the cream mixture, place a generous portion of chicken filling on it, and roll it up. Arrange the rolls in a baking pan, seam side down, and pour the remaining cream mixture over them. Top with the jack cheese and bake in the preheated oven for about 30 minutes.

Garnish with avocado, hard-boiled eggs, or olives.

Serves six.

BREASTS OF CHICKEN SUPRÊME

2 whole chicken breasts, boned, skinned, and cut in half
4 tablespoons butter
Salt and freshly ground black pepper
1 to 1½ cups buttered bread crumbs, as needed
4 slices baked ham
12 mushroom caps of uniform size
2 cups sauce suprême (page 238)
¼ cup sherry
Chopped parsley

Trim the chicken fillets nicely so they look neat and are of an even size. Sauté them gently in the butter till just cooked and lightly browned. Season with salt and pepper to taste, and roll in buttered crumbs.

Trim the ham slices so they are roughly the size of the fillets. Frizzle in the sauté pan just long enough to heat them through. Brush the mushroom caps with butter and broil until lightly browned.

Prepare the sauce suprême, stir in the sherry, and heat for a few moments more. Arrange the ham slices on a hot platter. Place a chicken fillet on each slice. Spoon the sauce over the fillets and top with mushrooms. Sprinkle with chopped parsley.

Serves four.

Variation

Arrange the sautéed fillets in a baking dish, top with sauce, sprinkle with buttered crumbs, grated Parmesan cheese, and paprika and brown quickly in a 350°F oven.

CREAMED CHICKEN WITH EGGS

This recipe is sometimes called Chicken Terrapin.

3 cups diced, cooked chicken
2 cups béchamel sauce (page 237), flavored with ¼ cup sherry
3 hard-boiled eggs, yolks and whites separated and chopped
Salt and freshly ground black pepper
6 slices toast
Chopped parsley

🐦 Heat the chicken in the top of a double boiler with the béchamel sauce flavored with sherry. Add the chopped egg yolks. Blend well, taste for seasoning, and serve on toast garnished with the chopped egg whites and parsley.

Serves six.

CHICKEN CRÊPES

3 cups chopped, cooked chicken
2 cups sauce suprême (page 238), flavored with 2 tablespoons Madeira
2 tablespoons finely chopped parsley
12 to 14 crêpes (see page 93)
Freshly grated Parmesan cheese

🐦 Mix the chicken, two-thirds of the sauce, and chopped parsley. Place a generous spoonful down the center of each crêpe, and roll. Arrange, seam side down, in a buttered 9 X 14-inch baking dish. Spoon the remaining sauce over the crêpes and sprinkle lightly with cheese. Bake in a 375°F oven till heated through and the cheese is lightly browned.

Serves six.

Basic Crêpes

   1 cup minus 2 tablespoons flour
   3 eggs
   4 to 5 tablespoons melted butter
   ⅛ teaspoon salt
   1 to 1¼ cups milk, or as needed

🥄 The crêpe batter can be made in an electric blender, food processor, or mixer; or in a bowl, using a rotary beater, hand electric beater, or wire whisk. First mix the flour, eggs, butter, and salt. Then gradually add milk until the batter has the consistency of light cream. Let the batter rest for 2 hours before using.

To make crêpes, butter a 6-inch pan with rounded sides, a crêpe pan if possible. Place the pan over medium-high heat. When the butter sizzles, pour a little batter into the pan, tilting and rotating so the batter coats the surface evenly. Pour any excess batter back into the bowl. Cook each crêpe until lightly browned on the underside, then turn and brown the other side. Remove from the pan and keep warm, covered with foil, until ready to use.

HOT CHICKEN SALAD

This is an admirable way to use leftover chicken, especially dark meat if you have served the breast of chicken the day before.

> 2 cups diced, cooked chicken
> ½ cup finely cut celery
> 2 tablespoons grated onion
> 2 tablespoons chopped parsley
> Salt and freshly ground black pepper
> Lemon juice to taste
> 1 cup béchamel sauce (page 237)
> 1 cup tart mayonnaise
> Paprika
> ¼ cup sliced almonds, toasted

Preheat the oven to 350°F.

Mix the chicken, celery, onion, and parsley. Season to taste with salt and pepper and a few drops of lemon juice. Prepare the béchamel sauce, and after it has cooled slightly, fold in the tart mayonnaise, made by whipping in an extra amount of lemon juice. Taste for seasoning, for this should have a decidedly tart flavor. You may need to add a few more drops of lemon juice. Arrange the chicken mixture in individual baking dishes or ramekins and top with the sauce. Dust with paprika and bake in the preheated oven for 10 to 15 minutes; the chicken should be heated through. Top with almonds and serve with peas and watermelon pickle.

Serves four.

Variation

You may add 1 tablespoon chopped green pepper or pimiento or 1 tablespoon finely cut sweet pickle to the chicken mixture for a different flavor.

CHICKEN IN LETTUCE LEAVES

This is a variation on an old Chinese recipe. Turkey may be used in place of the chicken.

3 cups cooked chicken
1½ cups finely chopped onions
¾ cup finely chopped green pepper
6 tablespoons butter
1 can (4 ounces) green chilies, seeded and finely chopped
1 to 2 tablespoons fresh hot chili pepper, finely chopped
1½ cups cooked rice
2 tablespoons chopped fresh basil or 1½ teaspoons dried
1 teaspoon salt
½ teaspoon freshly ground black pepper
½ cup Cognac
½ cup chicken broth, if needed
¼ cup chopped parsley
¾ cup toasted slivered almonds
2 heads chilled iceberg lettuce

❧ Cut the chicken into small dice. Sauté the onions and green peppers in butter over medium heat until they begin to soften; do not brown. Add the chilies, hot pepper, rice, and chicken, and toss well. Cover and cook over low heat for 4 to 5 minutes. Then add the basil, salt, pepper, Cognac, and chicken broth, if additional moisture is needed. Taste for seasoning and heat through.

Place in a bowl and garnish with parsley and almonds. Arrange chilled lettuce leaves in another serving dish. Invite guests to serve themselves: spoon some of the chicken mixture onto a cold lettuce leaf and roll it up.

Serves eight to ten.

Chicken Pies

FRENCH CHICKEN PIE

6 to 8 chicken legs with thighs, according to size
Flour for dredging
6 tablespoons butter
4 hard-boiled eggs, shelled and halved
3 to 4 slices bacon, cut in small pieces
2 onions, finely chopped
1 clove garlic, crushed
1 bay leaf
1 teaspoon dried thyme
½ pound mushrooms, sliced
¼ cup white wine
Salt and freshly ground black pepper to taste
Pastry of your choice for 1 crust
1 egg, beaten with 1 tablespoon cream

Dust the chicken pieces lightly with flour and brown on all sides in butter in a sauté pan. Arrange in a round baking dish with the hard-boiled eggs. Add the bacon, onions, garlic, and herbs to the sauté pan. Cook until the onions are just soft, then add the mushrooms and wine. Season with salt and pepper, cover, and simmer for 45 minutes. Pour the mixture in the pan over the chicken; allow to cool.

Roll out the pastry to fit the top of the dish. Cut a vent in the middle and place a small funnel of waxed paper in it to let the steam escape. Brush the pastry with the egg-cream mixture and bake in a 375°F oven for 25 to 30 minutes, or until the crust is thoroughly cooked.

To serve, cut a wedge of crust and set aside. Extract a leg and half an egg and put them on a warm plate. Spoon some of the bacon, mushrooms, and juices over them, and top with the wedge of crust.

Serves six.

PENNSYLVANIA CHICKEN PIE

1 chicken, 3 pounds
½ lemon
Boiling salted water to cover
1 medium onion, stuck with 3 cloves
Celery leaves
12 small white onions, peeled
6 carrots, scraped and quartered
16 potato balls or very small new potatoes, peeled
Salt and freshly ground black pepper
Chopped parsley
Pinch of dried marjoram
Béchamel sauce (page 237), using 1 cup combined chicken and
    vegetable broth
Rich pastry of your choice for 1 crust

Rub the inside of the chicken with half a lemon. Place in a pot
and cover with salted, boiling water. Add the onion stuck with the
cloves and a few celery leaves, cover loosely, and simmer until tender. Cool in the broth. Strip the meat from the bones and cut into
small chunks; reserve the broth.

In a separate pan, cook the small onions, carrots, and potatoes in
water to cover until tender. Drain, saving the broth, and season
with salt and pepper to taste.

Preheat the oven to 450°F.

Arrange the chicken and vegetables in an ovenproof casserole or
baking dish. Season with salt and pepper, and sprinkle with
chopped parsley and a pinch of marjoram. Make the béchamel
sauce, using 1 cup of combined chicken and vegetable broth, and
pour over the chicken. Cool. Cover with rich pastry and bake in the
preheated oven for 10 minutes. Reduce the heat to 375°F and continue baking till the pastry is cooked, about 30 minutes.

Serves six.

OLD-FASHIONED CHICKEN PIE

1 roasting chicken, 5 pounds, cut up,
  or an equivalent amount of chicken parts
1 medium onion
Celery leaves
1 bay leaf
Water to cover
Salt and freshly ground black pepper
12 small white onions, peeled
4 carrots, scraped and quartered
3 tablespoons flour
3 tablespoons butter
1 cup light cream or half-and-half
Pinch of freshly ground nutmeg
Chopped parsley
Paprika
Biscuit crust or flaky pastry of your choice

🐦 Place the chicken in a kettle with the onion, a few celery leaves, bay leaf, and water to cover. Cover tightly and simmer till tender, about 45 minutes. Salt and pepper the broth to taste.

In a separate pan, cook the white onions and carrots in water to cover till just tender. Drain and add salt to taste. Prepare a sauce by blending the flour and butter in a saucepan over low heat. Add 2 cups of the chicken broth and stir till thickened. Add the light cream and blend well. Season to taste with salt and a pinch of nutmeg.

Arrange the chicken and vegetables in a baking dish. Pile higher in the center of the dish or place an ovenproof egg cup or regular cup in the center to hold up the crust. Cover with the sauce and sprinkle with chopped parsley and paprika. Cool. Top with a biscuit crust or pastry, as you wish. Make a large vent in the crust to permit the steam to escape, or insert a funnel of brown paper or foil. For biscuit crust, bake in a 425°F oven for 20 to 25 minutes. For pastry, bake at 450°F for 10 minutes, then reduce the heat to 375°F and continue baking till the pastry is cooked.

Cole slaw is a natural with this dish.

Serves six to eight.

SPECIAL CHICKEN PIE

Rich pastry of your choice for 2 crusts, rolled very thin
3 whole chicken breasts, boned, skinned, and cut in half
4 tablespoons butter
1 cup sliced mushrooms, sautéed in butter
2 tablespoons chopped parsley
2½ cups sauce suprême (page 238), flavored with
  3 tablespoons Cognac
1 cup sliced almonds, blanched

Preheat the oven to 450°F.

Line an 11 X 14-inch oblong pan or baking dish with half the thinly rolled rich pastry. Cut the remaining pastry into strips and reserve. Separate each chicken fillet into 2 pieces and pound between sheets of waxed paper or foil. Sauté for a few seconds on each side in the butter to merely color. Arrange in the baking dish. Add the sautéed mushrooms and chopped parsley. Pour over this the sauce suprême flavored with the Cognac. Arrange the reserved strips of pastry over the pan in lattice fashion. Sprinkle with the almonds. Bake in the preheated 450°F oven for 10 minutes, then reduce the heat to 375°F and continue cooking till the pastry is crisp and brown. Cut in squares and serve.

Serves six.

CHICKEN OR TURKEY QUICHE

Pastry of your choice for a 9-inch pan 1½ inches deep
2 whole eggs plus 3 yolks
¾ cup milk
¾ cup heavy cream
1 tablespoon chopped fresh tarragon or ½ teaspoon dried
¾ teaspoon salt
¼ to ½ teaspoon freshly ground black pepper
2 cups cooked chicken or turkey, cut into dice

Roll out the pastry and prebake the shell in a 425°F oven for 15 to 20 minutes, until it is set and the edges begin to brown. Brush with 1 beaten yolk and return to the oven for another 2 minutes to dry the yolk and seal the crust. Beat the whole eggs and remaining yolks together, stir in the milk and cream, and add the tarragon and seasonings. Spread the diced chicken in the baked shell, and pour in the custard mixture. Bake at 350°F for about 30 minutes, or until the custard is set but still a bit runny at the center.

Serves four to six.

Chicken Salads

CHICKEN MAYONNAISE

This is the father and mother of all chicken salads and used to be a standard supper dish for summer.

Cut cold roasted or poached chicken in convenient portions for serving, and remove all the skin. Roll each piece in well-flavored mayonnaise to coat thoroughly. Arrange on a platter and garnish with sliced hard-boiled eggs, stuffed olives, and capers. Dust with chopped parsley. Surround the dish with tomato wedges and sliced cucumbers.

This dish is equally good made with cold duck or turkey.

SIMPLE CHICKEN SALAD

Cut up the meat of a cold chicken in generous-sized cubes. Blend with a well-flavored homemade olive oil mayonnaise (page 240). Arrange on crisp leaves of romaine and garnish with sliced blanched almonds and chopped parsley. That's all there is to it.

TRADITIONAL CHICKEN SALAD

The basic proportions of this salad are 2 cups diced, cooked chicken to 1 cup finely cut celery. Season with salt and freshly ground black pepper to taste and bind with mayonnaise. To serve traditionally, decorate with mayonnaise, sliced hard-boiled eggs, and capers.

Four cups of chicken salad will serve five people. If you are going into quantity feeding—a large supper party, for instance—you may stretch it a bit with more celery.

Thus, for 25 people you will want 3 quarts of diced chicken and 1½ quarts diced celery. For 50 people you will want 6 quarts chicken to 3 quarts celery.

Variations

Add to 2 cups diced cooked chicken:

1. 1½ cups cooked green beans marinated in a vinaigrette dressing. Mix with the chicken. Top with mayonnaise and decorate with tomato quarters.
2. ½ cup celery, ½ cup sliced ripe olives, ½ cup shaved toasted almonds. Bind with mayonnaise and decorate with almonds and olives.
3. 1 cup cold cooked green peas marinated in vinaigrette dressing. Bind with mayonnaise and decorate with raw peas.
4. 1 cup lightly toasted English walnut meats. Bind with mayonnaise and decorate with pimiento strips.
5. 1 cup coarsely chopped hard-boiled eggs, 2 tablespoons chopped sweet pickle, 2 tablespoons chopped parsley. Bind with mayonnaise.
6. 1 cup diced cooked sweetbreads, ½ cup diced cucumbers. Bind with mayonnaise and decorate with sliced cucumbers.
7. 1 cup seedless white grapes, ½ cup sliced almonds. Bind with mayonnaise and decorate with preserved kumquats.
8. 1 cup diced avocado. Dress with Russian dressing and decorate with ripe olives.
9. 1 cup finely cut celery. Bind with mayonnaise and decorate with asparagus tips. Use 4 to 6 tips for each person.
10. 1½ cups cold cooked rice marinated in 1 cup vinaigrette dressing and 1 tablespoon grated onion, 1 tablespoon chopped chives, 2 tablespoons chopped parsley, 2 tablespoons chopped green pepper, 1 tablespoon chopped pimiento and ½ cup chopped ripe olives. Dress with additional vinaigrette dressing.

Chicken Sandwiches

MY FAVORITE CHICKEN SANDWICH

Take thin slices of good white bread—homemade, if you have it—otherwise a home-style bread. Butter them well, place a generous supply of thinly sliced chicken on the slices, and sprinkle with salt. Press the slices together. Mayonnaise may be added if you like.

For luncheon sandwiches, use slices of bread ¼ inch thick. For tea and cocktail sandwiches, the bread should be so thin it resembles lace. Cut sandwiches into neat squares or fingers and let them chill, covered with a damp tea towel or cheesecloth, in the refrigerator for an hour or two before serving.

CLUB HOUSE SANDWICH

It may seem superfluous to include this veteran, but it is so often badly or incorrectly made that it could stand reviewing.

For each sandwich
  2 slices crisp, hot buttered toast
  3 or 4 slices crisp, hot bacon
  4 slices peeled ripe tomato
  Chicken slices, as many as you want
  Mayonnaise
  Lettuce (optional)

 Construct in this order: toast, chicken, tomato, mayonnaise, bacon, lettuce, toast. The mayonnaise then holds the bacon and prevents slipping and sliding. Green olives and sweet pickles are the traditional accompaniments.

To serve at a large party have the toasters going, arrange plates of the other makings, and let everyone do his or her own construction work.

COMPOSED SANDWICH

This sandwich makes a wonderful meal. One of its variations is the stalwart Reuben sandwich. Here is the basic recipe.

2 large slices Russian rye bread or pumpernickel, well buttered
3 or 4 thick slices of chicken or turkey
3 thin slices Swiss cheese
2 slices baked Virginia ham or smoked tongue
3 slices tomato
4 thin slices dill pickle
Russian dressing

Variations
1. Add cole slaw and Bermuda onion.
2. Use sliced American cheese instead of Swiss.
3. Add crisp bacon slices.
4. Add sauerkraut.

TOASTED CHICKEN SANDWICH

Remove the crusts from crisp hot toast. Butter well and quickly add thin slices of chicken. A little mayonnaise is acceptable here. Sweet pickles, too, seem to have an affection for toasted chicken sandwiches.

CHICKEN SALAD SANDWICH

Choose among the chicken salads given on pages 101–102 to use as a filling. Spread on buttered slices of bread. Naturally, the quality of the sandwich will depend on the quality of the bread. Use home-made, if possible. This sandwich is especially good on thin slices of buttered rye.

Chicken Hash, Croquettes, Soufflés

SUPERB CHICKEN HASH

1 large onion, finely chopped
2 green peppers, seeded and diced
5 tablespoons butter
2 tablespoons cooking oil
4 cups or more diced, cooked chicken
Salt and freshly ground black pepper to taste
Tabasco to taste
1½ teaspoons dried tarragon
½ cup chopped parsley
½ cup blanched almonds or broken walnut meats
8 eggs, lightly beaten
¾ cup freshly grated Parmesan cheese

✒ Sauté the onion and green pepper in the butter and oil until just wilted. Add the chicken and mix well. Add the seasonings, herbs, and almonds, and toss. Press the chicken down well in the skillet, cover, and cook over medium heat for 2 or 3 minutes. When the chicken is heated through, pour in the beaten eggs mixed with the cheese and cook over low heat until set. If practicable, place under the broiler for 2 or 3 minutes to brown.

Serves six.

SIMPLE CHICKEN HASH

2 to 3 cups leftover chicken pieces
Stuffing (if available)
1 medium onion, chopped very fine
4 tablespoons butter or bacon fat
2 tablespoons chopped parsley
Salt and freshly ground black pepper
Freshly grated nutmeg to taste
½ cup heavy cream

Cut the chicken into small dice or chop coarsely. If there is any stuffing left, add up to 1 cup to the chicken and blend well. Sauté the onion in the butter or fat. Add the chicken, stuffing, and parsley and mix thoroughly. Season with salt and pepper to taste and add a few grains of nutmeg. Pour in the cream and let it cook down till the hash has formed a pleasant brown crust at the bottom of the pan. Fold over with a spatula and serve with a green salad and some watermelon pickles. This recipe can also be made with leftover turkey.

Serves four to six.

CHICKEN HASH IN CREAM

This recipe may also be used as a filling for crêpes.

4 tablespoons butter
2 cups diced, cooked chicken
2 tablespoons chopped parsley
2 tablespoons grated onion
Salt and freshly ground black pepper
1 cup light béchamel sauce (page 237)
Buttered bread crumbs

Melt the butter in a heavy-bottomed skillet over a low flame. Add the chicken, parsley, and onion and toss well in the pan. Season with salt and pepper to taste and simmer till the chicken is thoroughly heated and slightly browned. Add the béchamel sauce and let simmer for 5 minutes. Sprinkle with buttered crumbs and serve with hot cornbread.

Serves four.

CHICKEN CROQUETTES

2 cups finely chopped, cooked chicken
1 tablespoon chopped parsley
Salt and freshly ground black pepper
Pinch of freshly grated nutmeg
1 cup thick béchamel sauce (page 237)
Flour for dredging
2 eggs, lightly beaten
1 cup finely grated fresh bread crumbs, or as needed
Fat for deep frying

Combine the chicken, parsley, and seasonings with the béchamel sauce. Allow to cool. Refrigerate for 2 to 3 hours.

With floured hands, shape the chilled chicken mixture into 10 or 12 balls or rolls. Dip in flour, then in beaten egg, and then in crumbs. Fry for approximately 3 minutes in deep fat, a few at a time, at a temperature of 370°F. Serve with sauce suprême (page 238).

Variations

1. Substitute 1 cup finely chopped raw mushrooms for 1 cup of the chicken.
2. Add 1 tablespoon grated onion and 1 teaspoon chopped fresh tarragon to the mixture.
3. Substitute ½ cup chopped almonds or walnuts for ½ cup of the chicken.

CHICKEN SOUFFLÉ

4 tablespoons butter

¼ cup flour

1½ cups milk or chicken stock

2 cups finely ground, cooked chicken

Salt and freshly ground black pepper

Pinch of freshly grated nutmeg

6 eggs, separated

❧ Preheat the oven to 350°F.

Make a thick béchamel sauce using the butter, flour, and milk (see page 237). When thickened, add the finely ground chicken, salt and pepper to taste, and nutmeg. Cool slightly, then add the egg yolks, beaten. Heat over hot, not boiling, water till the mixture is thickened. Cool again. Beat the egg whites stiff and fold in; pour the mixture into a buttered 2-quart soufflé dish. Bake in a pan of hot water in the preheated oven for 30 to 40 minutes, till puffed and brown. Serve at once.

Serves four.

Variations

1. Substitute 1 cup mushrooms, finely chopped and sautéed, for 1 cup of the chicken.
2. Add 3 tablespoons sherry to the sauce.

☙

Chicken Giblets

CHICKEN LIVERS EN BROCHETTE

Clean chicken livers and separate each into 2 pieces. Roll in thin slices of partially cooked bacon and secure on metal skewers, allowing 4 or 5 livers to a serving. Broil under a low flame till the bacon is crisp, turning the skewers frequently so the bacon is evenly cooked. Serve on a bed of parsley.

These also make a good accompaniment to drinks, in which case fasten each piece of liver and bacon with toothpicks or small bamboo skewers.

Variation

Marinate the livers in soy sauce, chopped garlic, and grated fresh ginger before wrapping in bacon.

SAUTÉ OF CHICKEN LIVERS

3 or 4 shallots, finely chopped
4 tablespoons butter
1 pound chicken livers, cleaned and separated into 2 pieces each
2 tablespoons chopped parsley
Salt and freshly ground black pepper
4 slices crisp toast

Sauté the shallots for 3 or 4 minutes in the butter. Add the chicken livers and sauté gently till nicely browned and cooked through. Add the chopped parsley and salt and pepper to taste. Serve on crisp toast.

Serves four.

Variations

1. These sautéed livers may be folded into an omelet for four.
2. Serve on a bed of buttered and well-flavored noodles, and add a bit of nutmeg as well as salt and pepper.

GIBLET SAUTÉ

½ pound chicken gizzards
3 or 4 chicken hearts, coarsely chopped
5 tablespoons butter
½ pound chicken livers, cut in 2 pieces each
1 tablespoon grated onion
2 tablespoons chopped parsley
1 tablespoon chopped chives
Salt and freshly ground black pepper

Simmer the gizzards and hearts for 25 minutes in boiling water. Drain. Melt 4 tablespoons of the butter in a skillet. Add the gizzards, cut into halves or quarters, hearts, and livers. Cook over a low flame, tossing well, till browned and well blended. Add the onion, parsley, and chives, season with salt and pepper to taste and add the remaining butter. Increase the heat to moderate and cook for 2 minutes, stirring well. Serve over rice or well-buttered noodles.

Serves four.

Variation

Chopped Giblet Sandwich: Sauté the gizzards, hearts, and livers in butter as directed above. Chop medium-fine in a wooden chopping bowl and add more chopped parsley and a bit more onion if desired. Add a dash of Tabasco. Spread on slices of well-buttered toast, and top with additional toast.

CHICKEN LIVER AND PORK PÂTÉ

½ pound chicken livers
4 tablespoons butter
2 eggs
½ cup Cognac or bourbon
1 medium onion, finely chopped
2 cloves garlic, finely chopped
½ teaspoon allspice
2 teaspoons salt
½ teaspoon freshly ground black pepper
1 teaspoon crushed rosemary
1 pound ground pork or sausage meat
¼ cup flour
Salt pork strips

Sauté the chicken livers over medium heat in the butter until they are just barely cooked and brown on all sides. Blend in a food processor with the eggs, Cognac, onion, garlic, seasonings, and rosemary. Mix with the ground pork and flour. Put into a 9 X 5 inch loaf pan or pâté mold lined with salt pork strips. Cover with foil or a lid. Bake in a 350°F oven for 1½ to 2 hours, or until the liquid and fat are clear. Allow to cool for about 20 minutes, then weight down and cool completely.

Serves eight to ten.

QUICK CHICKEN LIVER PÂTÉ

½ pound chicken livers
4 tablespoons butter, plus 2 tablespoons for top
2 hard-boiled eggs
¼ cup Cognac
½ pound cream cheese
1 small truffle, diced

Sauté the livers over medium heat in the butter until barely cooked and brown on all sides, then cool. Place in a food processor with the eggs and Cognac, and blend until smooth. Mix thoroughly with the cream cheese. Pack into a small (2–2½-cup) bowl or terrine, sprinkle with the diced truffle, and cover with a thin layer of melted butter. Refrigerate until ready to serve.

CHOPPED CHICKEN LIVERS

2 pounds chicken fat
3 large onions, finely chopped
Salt and freshly ground black pepper
1½ pounds chicken livers

Dice the chicken fat, and render in a heavy skillet. When the fat liquifies and cracklings form, add ½ cup of the onions and cook until they are browned. Strain through cheesecloth and reserve both the fat and the crackling-onion residue. Heat 4 tablespoons of melted fat in a heavy pot, add the remaining uncooked onions, and cover the pot. Cook over low heat until the onions are limp and slightly colored. Sprinkle with salt and pepper.

Heat the rest of the melted chicken fat in the skillet, and sauté the livers until they are just cooked through. Remove and chop quite fine. Blend with the pan juices and crackling-onion mixture, and season to taste with salt and pepper. For a finer texture, put the mixture through a grinder. Serve chilled with matzohs or other crackers.

Fresh Cornish Game Hen

Cornish game hen can be prepared in many of the ways suggested for chicken but is especially good roasted or sautéed. However, I recommend using only fresh birds. These young hens, five to six weeks old, range from 1 to 1¾ pounds and are delicate in flavor and tender. They are also far less expensive than domestic game birds like quail and partridge. Plan to serve one game hen per person.

ROAST CORNISH GAME HEN

Rub inside and out with half a lemon, brush well with oil, and season with salt and pepper (or use one of the treatments suggested for roast chicken), and roast in a 425°F oven for 22 minutes, brushing with additional oil after 10 minutes. Don't be afraid to use your fingers to eat these delicious birds.

ROAST STUFFED CORNISH GAME HEN

1 game hen per person
½ lemon

For each bird

⅓ cup chopped onion or shallot
1 tablespoon butter
⅔ cup fresh bread crumbs
Melted butter
Salt and freshly ground black pepper
Tarragon, rosemary, or thyme—fresh or dried
Dash of Cognac or Madeira

❧ Rub each bird inside and out with half a lemon. Sauté the chopped onion or shallot in the tablespoon of butter. Add the bread crumbs and enough melted butter to moisten them. Season with salt and pepper, and add your choice of herb and a dash of Cognac or Madeira. Blend all ingredients, and stuff each bird. Skewer the vents or close with a piece of foil, truss (see page 57), and roast on a rack in a 350°F oven for 30 to 35 minutes.

DIETER'S ROAST STUFFED CORNISH GAME HEN

1 game hen per person

For each bird
2 strips bacon
1 small onion, chopped
6 small green pitted olives
1 teaspoon dried tarragon
Salt and freshly ground black pepper

❧ Cut one slice of bacon into small pieces and combine with the chopped onion, olives, and tarragon. Place in the cavity of the bird. Arrange the second piece of bacon across the breast, and season with salt and pepper. Set the bird on a rack in a shallow pan, and roast at 350°F for 30 to 35 minutes.

SAUTÉED CORNISH GAME HEN

Split each bird in half and sauté quickly in butter and oil for about 8 to 10 minutes on each side; or use one of the treatments suggested for sautéed chicken.

BROILED CORNISH GAME HEN

Split each bird down the back and flatten to provide more even cooking. Brush with oil and season with salt and pepper (or use one of the treatments suggested for broiled chicken) and broil 4 inches under moderate heat about 8 to 10 minutes on each side.

Chicken Broths and Soups

Chicken broth or stock has many uses in the kitchen. It can be served clear or in combination with other ingredients for soup; it forms the basis for many other soups and can be used for sauces and aspics, as an additive to braised dishes, and for cooking certain vegetables. Most good cooks keep a supply of it frozen. For general purposes, use backs, necks, and gizzards rather than other chicken parts or a whole chicken. Not only is this more economical, but it provides good flavor and can be cooked down without regard for the meat.

BASIC CHICKEN BROTH

4 pounds chicken backs, necks, and gizzards
3 quarts water
Celery tops or 1 or 2 stalks celery
1 medium onion, stuck with 2 cloves
1 sprig parsley
1 clove garlic
6 peppercorns
Salt to taste, or about 1 tablespoon

Place the chicken parts and gizzards in a soup kettle and add the water, celery, onion, parsley, garlic, and peppercorns. Bring slowly to a boil and skim off any scum that forms. Reduce the heat, cover, and simmer gently for 2 to 2½ hours. Add salt to taste and strain through a linen cloth or filter paper. Allow to cool, and skim off the fat.

Variations

1. Combine with an equal amount of tomato juice and a pinch of cayenne pepper. Heat and serve.
2. *Cream Soup:* Add 2 egg yolks and 1 cup cream, lightly beaten together, for each 4 cups of broth. Stir constantly over low heat

till the soup is of a desired thickness; do not allow to boil. Season to taste and garnish with bits of shredded chicken and chopped parsley.

3. *Noodle Soup:* Cook 4 ounces of egg noodles with 1 quart of broth and add shreds of chicken.

4. Add 1 tablespoon of Madeira or sherry to each cup of soup.

CHICKEN CONSOMMÉ

5 to 6 pounds chicken backs, necks, and gizzards
1 veal knuckle
2 pounds shin of beef with bone
1 onion, stuck with 3 cloves
2 to 3 carrots
3 sprigs parsley
2 celery tops or 2 stalks celery
1 clove garlic
¼ teaspoon dried thyme
1 tablespoon salt
1 tablespoon peppercorns
4 quarts cold water
3 egg whites

～ You will need an 8- or 10-quart kettle for this soup. Combine all the ingredients (except the egg white). Bring to a boil, and skim off any scum that forms. Then turn the heat low and cover so the broth simmers very gently for 4 or 5 hours, adding hot water if there is too much evaporation. Strain off the broth. Let it cool. Then skim off all fat.

To clarify (for 2 to 3 quarts broth): Be sure the pot in which you clarify is spotlessly clean. Pour the broth into the pot. Beat the egg whites to soft peaks and add to the broth. Whisk over medium heat until the broth comes to a boil. Reduce the heat and simmer for 15 minutes, then allow to stand for 10 to 12 minutes. Strain through a linen cloth or several thicknesses of filter paper. (Coffee filters work very well.)

To serve: This may be served clear or with any of the following: egg or spinach noodles; rice; thin slices of soft, ripe avocado added just before serving; a touch of Madeira or sherry; tiny croutons of bread, fried in butter; chopped chives and parsley; tarragon and white wine; chopped hard-boiled egg and paprika; chopped raw spinach; rounds of toasted, buttered bread sprinkled with grated Parmesan cheese.

The broth or consommé may be frozen and used as you need it.

Serves eight.

CRÈME VICHYSSOISE

This popular soup was created in New York by the famous chef Louis Diat. The following recipe is my own version. Essentially, this is a leek and potato soup, served cold.

8 to 10 leeks
3 tablespoons butter or chicken fat
3 cups chicken broth, or as needed
4 medium mealy potatoes, peeled
Salt and freshly ground black pepper to taste
½ teaspoon freshly grated nutmeg
1¼ cups sweet or sour cream or yogurt, or to taste
Chopped chives

❧ Cut the green tops from the leeks and save for flavoring other soups. Cut the white part into 1-inch lengths and clean thoroughly under cold running water. In butter or chicken fat, sauté the white part of the leeks gently, being careful not to brown. When wilted, add 1 cup chicken broth and simmer gently. Meanwhile, boil the potatoes in salted water.

When the potatoes and leeks are tender, combine them, add another 1 cup chicken broth, and let them simmer together for 10 minutes. Crush the potatoes with a fork so they become saturated with the leek flavor. Season with salt and pepper to taste and add the nutmeg.

Force the vegetables through a fine sieve or food mill with the broth. Add another 1 cup broth, or more if the vegetable purée seems too thick. When it is cool, place it in the refrigerator and chill it for 18 to 24 hours.

The last step is to add cream, sour cream, or yogurt to the purée. You will need about 1½ cups of cream to each quart of purée. But that is really something you will have to work out for your own taste. Be sure that the soup is well chilled when served. Top each serving with chopped chives or pass the chives separately.

Serves six.

Variations

1. *Curried:* Add 1 teaspoon or more, according to your taste, of curry powder to the purée when it is still hot. This is relished by a great many people. You may also use chopped fresh coriander, if you like its flavor, instead of chives.

2. *With cucumber:* Peel and split a crisp cucumber. Remove all seeds and cut in rather thin half-moons. Fold into the soup an hour or so before serving.

3. *Apple Vichyssoise:* Thin shreds or slices of tart apple may be combined with the soup an hour before serving.

A RICH CREAM OF CHICKEN SOUP

1 chicken, 4 pounds
2 or 3 leeks
1 onion, stuck with 3 cloves
Celery tops
1 tablespoon peppercorns
Cold water to cover
Salt and finely ground black pepper
1½ cups cream, blended with 3 egg yolks
2 tablespoons sherry
Blanched almonds (optional)

Choose a good plump chicken. Place it in a pot with the leeks, the onion stuck with the cloves, several celery tops, and the peppercorns. Cover with cold water and simmer till tender. Remove the meat from the breast and reserve. Return the carcass with the remaining meat to the broth; simmer another hour. Remove the carcass. Season the broth to taste, skim off the fat, and strain through cheesecloth.

Strip the meat from the carcass and put through a food processor or chop very fine. Add the chopped meat to the strained broth, heat thoroughly, and add the cream and egg yolks. Do not allow to boil. Stir constantly till the soup is slightly thickened; add the sherry. Cut the breast meat into julienne and add to the soup. Thinly shaved almonds may be used as a garnish.

Serves six.

CHICKEN-MUSHROOM SOUP

½ pound mushrooms, very thinly sliced
3 tablespoons butter
3 cups chicken broth
Salt to taste
1 cup hot cream, blended with 2 egg yolks
3 tablespoons Madeira

Sauté the mushrooms in the butter, reserving a mushroom cap for each serving. When soft but not browned—about 5 minutes—add the chicken broth and simmer gently till heated through. Add salt to taste and the hot cream blended with the egg yolks. Stir constantly over low heat till the soup is slightly thickened; do not allow to boil. Add the Madeira. Garnish each cup with a broiled mushroom cap.

Serves six.

COLD PEA SOUP

½ cup soaked green split peas
3 cups chicken broth
Salt and freshly ground black pepper to taste
1 cup heavy cream or yogurt
Finely chopped fresh mint

Simmer the soaked split peas in the chicken broth till tender. Force through a fine sieve and season to taste with salt and pepper. Chill for 24 hours and combine with cream or yogurt. Chill again for an hour before serving and serve with finely chopped mint.

Serves four.

CHAPTER 2

Turkey

The national holiday bird is now with us the year round and is as readily available in markets as chicken. Like chicken, it is being sold in parts, providing the chance to enjoy turkey for a meal or two without facing a week of leftovers. Turkey breasts are good buys for small families who prefer white meat; and dark meat fanciers can indulge themselves in legs and thighs. In addition, whole turkeys for roasting are produced in a tremendous range of sizes, from 4 or 5 pounds to 30 pounds and over. Many of these come with fat inserted under the skin for self-basting, and others come boned and rolled. While frozen birds dominate, it is still possible to find fresh-killed turkeys throughout the country.

Turkey is being used in more imaginative ways than ever before, but the classic preparation is still that of roasting. Unfortunately there are no definitive rules to guide the inexperienced cook, but after a lifetime of turkey, this is the procedure I now recommend.

BASIC ROAST TURKEY

1 turkey, 18 to 20 pounds
½ lemon
Stuffing of your choice (see pages 227–236)
8 tablespoons or more softened butter
Salt and freshly ground black pepper
Strips of fresh siding or larding pork, or bacon rind

❧ Preheat the oven to 350°F.

Rub the inside of the turkey with half a lemon, and dry with paper towels. Fill the body and neck cavities with stuffing, but not too tightly—the crumbs should remain somewhat loose. Place a piece of folded foil over the stuffing in the vent, then secure the neck skin and vent with skewers, and truss (see page 125). Massage the skin well with the softened butter, then salt and pepper it.

Line a roasting rack with strips of siding, larding pork, or bacon rind, which you can sometimes buy from your butcher when he cuts down a whole slab. Set the rack in a fairly shallow roasting pan and place the turkey, breast side down, on the rack. Roast for 1 hour in the preheated oven, then turn the turkey on its side (to turn the bird, I use wads of paper towels), and rub with butter. Roast for another hour. Turn on its other side, and rub with butter. Roast for a third hour. Turn the turkey on its back and rub the breast with butter. Return to the oven and continue roasting till the turkey tests done. Remove from the oven and place on a hot platter. Allow the bird to rest for 15 minutes if being served hot. If being served tepid, let it cool gently at room temperature. Remove all the twine and skewers. Proceed to carve.

Serves sixteen or more.

STUFFING

Stuff both the vent and neck cavity of the bird, using approximately ½ – ¾ cup of stuffing per pound. Do not pack, but fill loosely. If you like, use one type of stuffing for the vent and another for the neck— for example, a bread stuffing and a sausage stuffing. Draw the neck skin over the stuffing and tie it well or secure with skewers. Sew up the vent or arrange a piece of folded foil over the stuffing and skewer the opening.

TRUSSING

Turn the wing tips under the back of the turkey. Using a long piece of kitchen string, tie the legs together, wrap around the tail, and then secure the legs and tail together, leaving two lengths of string. Cross these under the middle of the back, wrap around each wing, bring together over the breast and tie. To keep the legs closer to the body, insert a skewer in the joint between each leg and thigh. Tie a piece of string from one skewer to the other, running it under the back.

TESTING

The trick of roasting a turkey is to keep the white meat from becoming dry while cooking the dark meat sufficiently. There is no certain test to tell you when the turkey is done, and you must rely a good bit on your judgment. Here are two general rules to help you. First, see if the leg can be moved up and down *somewhat* flexibly. (To my mind, by the time the leg is really loose, the bird is overdone.) Second, prick the leg joint with a fork: if the juices run clear or faintly pink, the bird is done.

Variations

1. *With garlic and black pepper:* Stuff the turkey with a 6-inch length of dry French bread that has been rubbed with garlic to saturate it, and then rolled in freshly ground black pepper. This makes a fairly heady seasoning, and is especially good for small turkeys roasted on the spit.

2. *Truffled Turkey:* Use either the white Italian truffles or the black French variety. The night before roasting the turkey, cut the truffles in slices ⅛ inch thick. Loosen the breast skin with your fingers and arrange the truffle slices underneath. Also place several slices in the cavity of the bird if you are not stuffing it. Secure the neck and skin and vent, and truss (see page 125). Rub well with a mixture of salt, freshly ground black pepper, butter, and a little thyme. Follow basic roasting directions above.

TRADITIONAL ACCOMPANIMENTS FOR
ROAST TURKEY

Baked ham; grilled pork sausages of various kinds; puréed potatoes and puréed yellow turnips, either separate or mixed; creamed dried corn; roasted chestnuts or chestnut purée; baked or candied yams; braised celery; glazed onions; sauerkraut; cranberry sauce.

POLLY HAMBLET'S ROAST HALF TURKEY

Have a turkey split lengthwise. Freeze one half for another occasion, if you like. Fill the other half turkey with the stuffing of your choice (see pages 227–236) and lay, stuffed side down, on a well-buttered piece of cooking parchment or foil. Sear in a preheated oven at 475°F, then turn the heat down to 350°F and roast, allowing 15 minutes a pound. Baste every 15 minutes. The parchment or foil will enable you to lift the bird from the pan with the stuffing intact.

A half turkey of 8 pounds will serve six at dinner, with leftovers for the next day.

BONED AND ROLLED TURKEY

This makes an excellent buffet dish that can be served either hot or cold.

1 turkey, 10 to 12 pounds
1 cup finely chopped onions
½ cup finely chopped celery
6 tablespoons butter
1 tablespoon dried tarragon
½ cup finely chopped parsley
2 cups fresh bread crumbs
Optional: 1 cup finely chopped mushrooms, chopped cooked giblets, or
   chopped nuts
1 egg, lightly beaten
Salt and freshly ground black pepper

∿ Have your butcher bone the turkey for you, leaving only the drumsticks. Sauté the onions and celery in the butter until just wilted, then add the tarragon, parsley, bread crumbs, and any of the optional ingredients. Remove from the heat and mix with the beaten egg and seasonings.

Spread mixture on the inside of the turkey, roll tightly, and tie in several places to completely seal. Place on a rack in a roasting pan, brush with melted butter, and roast at 350°F for ½ to 2 hours, or until a meat thermometer registers 165°F at the center of the roll. Allow to cool slightly before cutting into slices.

Serves eight.

ROAST TURKEY BREAST

The average turkey breast available at the market comes from smaller turkeys and weighs about 2½ pounds, enough to serve up to four people. To serve more than that, try to locate a breast weighing about 4 to 5 pounds. Rub it well with butter, salt, freshly ground black pepper, and a little thyme or rosemary. Place on a rack, skin side down, and roast 13 to 15 minutes per pound in a 325°F oven. Baste frequently, turning once or twice.

Variation

Spit and balance the breast, and roast over medium coals, basting often with melted butter and a little thyme, allowing 15 minutes per pound, or until nicely browned and just tender.

TURKEY WINGS TERIYAKI

4 whole turkey wings, about 4¾ pounds
Cooking oil
⅔ cup soy sauce
¼ cup sweet sherry
2 tablespoons minced ginger root
2 large cloves garlic, minced
1 tablespoon grated orange rind

∾ Preheat the oven to 375°F.

Cut each wing into three portions at the joints, reserving the wing tips for use in stock at another time. Dip the remaining portions in oil and place in a single layer in a small roasting pan. Roast, uncovered, in the preheated oven for 45 minutes. Stir together the remaining ingredients and pour over the wings. Cover tightly with foil and continue baking at the same temperature until tender, about 45 minutes. Serve with rice.

Serves four.

TURKEY BROTH

Carcass from a roast turkey, plus neck and giblets (optional) and any
leftover skin
1 onion, stuck with 3 cloves
2 to 3 carrots, unpeeled
Celery leaves
1 clove garlic
½ teaspoon dried thyme
6 peppercorns
Cold water to cover
Salt

~ Place all the ingredients except the salt in a large kettle. Bring
to a boil and simmer for 2 hours, or until you have a rich, well-flavored broth; season to taste. Skim the fat off the broth and strain
through two thicknesses of cheesecloth.

Variation
Bring the broth to a boil. Add noodles, and cook gently until ten-
der. Serve with slices of hard-boiled egg and plenty of toasted
French bread.

POACHED TURKEY

Prepare a turkey as for roasting (see page 124). When the bird is
stuffed and trussed, wrap it securely in a heavily floured cloth and
tie it well. Place in a large kettle and cover with boiling, salted
water. Simmer for 3 to 3½ hours, according to the size of the bird.
Unwrap, remove strings and skewers, and serve surrounded by
grilled sausages.

A béchamel sauce (page 237) may be served with this. Add the
chopped cooked giblets and 3 tablespoons chopped parsley to the
sauce. Or serve with a hollandaise sauce (page 238) and steamed rice.

POACHED TURKEY IN PARCHMENT

Butter a turkey and secure 2 or 3 thin slices smoked ham to the breast. Place in a parchment cooking bag and tie securely. Place in a deep kettle and cover with boiling water. Simmer for 2 to 3 hours, according to the size of the bird. Serve hot with a giblet sauce or cold with a rémoulade sauce (page 217), cold sliced tongue, and cole slaw. With a decorative garnish, a cold poached turkey makes a handsome and unusual dish for a buffet.

BROILED TURKEY

Turkeys weighing from 3 to 6 pounds are best for broiling. Split them lengthwise, rub well with butter, and place, skin side down, on a broiling rack. Set about 3 inches from the heat in a broiler pre-heated to 350°F. Broil until nicely browned, basting frequently with melted butter. Turn, season with salt and freshly ground black pepper to taste, and brown well again, continuing to baste. This will take from 30 to 45 minutes.

One broiler will serve four to six, depending upon the size of the bird.

Variations

1. Add finely chopped, cooked giblets to the basting butter for the last 10 minutes of cooking.
2. Sprinkle heavily with chopped parsley when removed from broiler.
3. Baste with olive oil and chopped garlic.

BRAISED TURKEY

1 small turkey, about 8 to 10 pounds
8 tablespoons butter or butter and oil
Salt and freshly ground black pepper
2 cups broth, made from the neck and giblets
1 cup dry white wine
2 tablespoons chopped parsley

❧ Preheat the oven to 350°F.

Wipe the turkey with a damp cloth, and truss (page 57). Brown it quickly on all sides in the butter or butter and oil in a deep oven-proof casserole or roasting pan. Season with salt and pepper to taste. Add the broth (reserve the giblets) and the wine. Cover the casserole or roasting pan with cooking parchment or foil and tie securely; or cover with a lid and seal with a thick paste made with flour and water. Place in the preheated oven and cook till the turkey is tender, allowing 20 to 25 minutes per pound.

Remove the turkey to a hot platter, detaching all strings and skewers. Let the broth cook down very briskly. Degrease, and add the reserved cooked giblets, chopped, the parsley, and salt and pepper to taste. Serve with buttered noodles.

Serves six to eight.

BRAISED TURKEY WITH TRUFFLES

Truffles—fresh, if possible, as many as you can afford
1 turkey, 8 to 10 pounds
2 pounds ground pork
1½ pounds ground veal
8 shallots, chopped
Butter
Salt and freshly ground black pepper
¾ cup Cognac

2 cups fine bread crumbs

½ cup chopped parsley

3 carrots, cut into julienne

3 leeks, well cleaned and cut into julienne

3 stalks celery, cut into fine julienne

1½ cups dry white wine, plus additional for basting

Beurre manié (3 tablespoons flour and 3 tablespoons butter kneaded
  together)

❧ Slice several truffles and slip them under the breast skin of the
turkey. Place several more whole truffles in the cavity. Allow to
stand for at least 1 hour so the truffles perfume the bird, or refrigerate overnight, loosely wrapped in foil. Remove the truffles from the
cavity and chop finely.

Prepare the stuffing. Sauté the ground meats and shallots in 8
tablespoons butter until heated through, and add 2 teaspoons of salt
and ½ cup Cognac. Combine with the bread crumbs, parsley, and
chopped truffles. Taste for seasoning by lightly sautéing a small
piece, and add more salt if necessary, and black pepper. Stuff the
turkey lightly with this mixture, close the vent, and truss.

Brown the turkey in butter, or butter and oil, in a large skillet.
You can turn it by using wads of paper towels. Melt 4 tablespoons
butter in a deep braising pan, and in this make a bed of the carrots,
leeks, and celery. Arrange the turkey on the vegetables, breast side
up. Add the wine and bring it to a boil, then reduce to a simmer.
Cover the pan, and cook the turkey for 2½ to 3 hours, basting occasionally with a mixture of melted butter and white wine.

When the turkey is tender—the thigh juices run clear—transfer
to a hot platter. Remove excess fat from the pan and strain the
juices. If there is more than 2 cups, reduce over high heat. Thicken
with the beurre manié, worked into tiny balls and added a few at a
time. Adjust the seasoning, and stir in the remaining Cognac. Pass
separately with the carved turkey.

Serves eight to ten.

BRAISED TURKEY WINGS

4 pounds turkey wings, with tips removed
8 tablespoons butter or butter and oil
1 cup chicken or turkey broth
Salt and freshly ground black pepper to taste

🐦 Brown the turkey wings in butter or butter and oil in a heavy pot or flameproof casserole. Season to taste and add the broth. Cover tightly and cook over low heat for about 45 minutes, or until tender when tested with a fork. The wings can also be cooked in a 350°F oven.

Serves four.

Variations

1. *With white wine and tarragon:* Brown the wings in butter, then pour in ½ cup dry white wine and ½ cup chicken or turkey broth. Add 2 tablespoons fresh tarragon or 2 teaspoons dried, and salt lightly to taste. Cover and cook as directed above. Just before serving, add a few drops of freshly squeezed lemon juice.

2. *Provençal:* Brown the wings in 6 tablespoons olive oil. Add 1 can (1 pound) tomatoes, peeled, seeded, and chopped; 2 cloves garlic, finely chopped; 1 tablespoon chopped fresh basil or a pinch of dried thyme. Salt lightly to taste. Cover and cook as directed above.

3. *Chili:* Brown the turkey wings in 3 tablespoons butter and 3 tablespoons oil. Add 1 large onion, finely chopped; 2 or 3 cloves garlic, finely chopped; 1½ tablespoons chili powder; 1 hot pepper, cut in strips; ½ cup tomato paste; ½ cup chicken or turkey broth; ½ teaspoon dried basil; and a pinch of powdered coriander. Season with salt to taste. Cover and cook as directed above. Before serving, correct the seasoning and add a few ripe olives. If you like, thicken the sauce with beurre manié (bits of flour and butter kneaded together).

MABELLE'S TURKEY CASSEROLE

1 small turkey, about 7 pounds, cut up

Flour

Salt and freshly ground black pepper

8 tablespoons butter or butter and oil

½ pound bacon, diced

½ cup chopped shallots or green onion

2 cups turkey broth, made from the neck and giblets

~◆ Preheat the oven to 325°F.

Dredge turkey pieces with flour, salt, and pepper. Heat the butter or butter and oil in a large skillet and brown a few turkey pieces at a time. Transfer to a large ovenproof casserole. Add the bacon, chopped shallots or green onion, and broth. Cover the casserole and allow to simmer in the preheated oven for 1½ to 2 hours, or until the turkey is tender. Taste for seasoning. If you want, thicken the sauce with beurre manié (bits of flour and butter kneaded together). Serve with hot cornbread and succotash.

Serves six to eight.

Variations

1. Omit the bacon and shallots. Add ¼ teaspoon each freshly grated nutmeg and ground ginger. Use 3 cups red wine instead of broth. Just before serving, add 1 cup drained canned black cherries and 1 tablespoon grated lemon zest.
2. Twenty minutes before the turkey is done, add 3 tablespoons fresh tarragon leaves or 1 tablespoon dried soaked in white wine and drained.
3. Add 1 cup mushrooms sautéed in butter.
4. 25 minutes before the dish is done, remove the cover of the casserole and top the turkey with rounds of biscuit dough. Increase the heat to 425°F.

TURKEY AND WILD RICE CASSEROLE

1 cup wild rice

1 pound mushrooms, sliced

1 onion, chopped

6 tablespoons butter

3 cups diced, cooked turkey

½ cup sliced almonds, blanched

2 teaspoons salt

¼ teaspoon freshly ground black pepper

3½ cups turkey or chicken broth

1 cup heavy cream

3 tablespoons freshly grated Parmesan cheese

Wash the rice thoroughly and cover with boiling water. Let soak for 1 hour. Drain well.

Preheat the oven to 350°F.

Sauté the mushrooms and onion in 3 tablespoons butter for 10 minutes. Place in a buttered ovenproof casserole, along with the rice, turkey, almonds, and salt and pepper. Add the broth and cream; mix lightly. Cover and bake in the preheated oven for 1½ hours. Remove the cover, sprinkle with the cheese, and dot with the remaining butter. Increase the heat to 450°F and bake for 5 minutes longer.

Serves six to eight.

SCALLOPED TURKEY WITH NOODLES

8 ounces noodles
Slices of cooked turkey and stuffing
Hard-boiled eggs
2 cups thin béchamel sauce (page 237) or turkey gravy
Salt and freshly ground black pepper
Buttered bread crumbs

❧ Cook noodles in boiling, salted water till tender. Drain. In a buttered casserole, arrange alternating layers of noodles, turkey, and stuffing. Finish with a layer of sliced hard-boiled eggs. Pour béchamel sauce or turkey gravy over this and season to taste. Sprinkle with buttered crumbs and bake in a 400°F oven for 20 minutes.

Serves four.

TURKEY CASSEROLE WITH OLIVES

2 shallots, chopped, or sliced green onions
2 tablespoons butter
½ cup dry vermouth
½ cup pitted ripe olives
2 cups cooked turkey breast, diced
⅛ teaspoon thyme
⅛ teaspoon crushed rosemary
1 cup brown sauce (see p. 173)
Salt and freshly ground black pepper
A squeeze or 2 of lemon juice
1 package frozen peas, thawed

❧ In a pan, sauté the shallot or green onions in the butter until limp. Remove from heat, add the rest of the ingredients, and stir to blend well. Pour into a casserole, and bake at 350°F for 35 to 40 minutes.

Serves 4.

CASSEROLE OF TURKEY WITH RICE

7 tablespoons unsalted butter

2 medium onions, chopped

½ pound firm white mushrooms, sliced

2 cups diced, cooked turkey

½ cup diced baked ham

1 cup crumbled leftover bread stuffing

2 tablespoons chopped parsley

¼ teaspoon dried thyme

Salt and freshly ground black pepper

1 tablespoon curry powder

1 cup uncooked rice

2 cups hot chicken or turkey broth, or as needed

Melt 6 tablespoons butter in a skillet, add the onions, and sauté over medium heat until limp and golden. Add the mushrooms and sauté for 2 or 3 minutes, until just cooked through. Combine in an ovenproof casserole with the turkey, ham, stuffing, parsley, and thyme. Mix well and taste for seasoning. Add salt and pepper if necessary.

Preheat the oven to 375°F.

Melt the remaining tablespoon butter in the skillet, add the curry powder and rice, and sauté lightly over medium heat until the rice is just translucent (curry powder should always be cooked to take away the raw taste before being added to a dish). Add to the casserole, pour in the hot broth, cover the casserole, and bake until the rice is tender and the liquid absorbed—about 25 to 30 minutes. If the rice does not seem quite tender, add a little more heated broth and continue cooking.

Serves four to six.

TURKEY BREAST PAPPAGALLO

12 slices turkey breast, ⅜ inch thick

Flour

8 tablespoons butter

6 tablespoons oil

Salt and freshly ground black pepper

12 ham slices

8 small mushrooms, sliced and sautéed in butter

½ cup chicken or turkey broth

Freshly grated Parmesan cheese

Chopped parsley

~ Pound the turkey slices between sheets of waxed paper until very thin. Dust the slices in flour. Melt the butter in two skillets, add the oil, and sauté the turkey until delicately brown on both sides. Season with salt and pepper. Add a slice of ham to each piece of turkey and a tablespoon of mushrooms. Spoon the broth over this, and sprinkle with Parmesan cheese. Cover both skillets, reduce the heat, and simmer for about 5 minutes. Arrange the turkey on a hot platter, and distribute the pan juices over it. Garnish with chopped parsley.

Serves six.

TURKEY SALTIMBOCCA

12 small uncooked slices of turkey breast
4 shallots, finely chopped
6 tablespoons butter
½ cup duxelles (see Stuffings, p. 227)
2 tablespoons chopped fresh tarragon or 2 teaspoons dried
6 tablespoons grated Parmesan cheese
Flour
2 eggs, lightly beaten
Fresh bread crumbs
2 tablespoons oil
Dry white wine or chicken broth
½ cup sour cream or yogurt
1 tablespoon chopped parsley

Pound the slices of turkey breast between sheets of waxed paper into thin rounds about 2½ inches in diameter. Sauté the shallots in 2 tablespoons of butter until limp. Stir in the duxelles, and remove from the heat. Add the tarragon and cheese. Spread about 2 tablespoons of this mixture on a slice of turkey, and cover with a second piece. Press the edges firmly together. Dust with flour, dip in the beaten egg, and then in the bread crumbs. Place on a baking sheet lined with waxed paper, and refrigerate for 30 minutes to firm up.

Heat the remaining butter and oil in a heavy skillet, and sauté the the turkey pieces until cooked through and golden, about 2 minutes on a side. Remove to a warm platter.

Pour the wine or broth into the skillet and reduce over high heat. Turn off heat, stir in the sour cream or yogurt and chopped parsely. Pour over the saltimbocca.

Serves 6.

TURKEY CHILI

1 small turkey, 5 to 6 pounds, cut in quarters

1 onion stuck with cloves

2 stalks celery

2 or 3 sprigs parsley

2 small dried hot peppers

Salt

2 tablespoons chili powder

1 can (4 ounces) green chilies, seeded and finely chopped

1 cup ground almonds

½ cup ground peanuts

1 large onion, finely chopped

3 cloves garlic, finely chopped

2 green peppers, finely chopped

4 tablespoons olive oil

1 cup small green olives

½ cup blanched almonds

Cover the turkey with water in a deep pot, and add the onion, celery, parsley, and hot peppers. Bring to a boil and skim off any surface scum, then reduce the heat and cover the pot. Simmer until the turkey is tender but not falling from the bones, about 1 hour. Remove the turkey from the broth, and when it is cool enough to handle, strip the meat from the bones in good chunks.

Degrease the broth and reduce it by half over high heat until you have 4 cups. Strain it and add salt to taste. Then add the chili powder, green chilies, and ground nuts; simmer until well blended and thickened. Sauté the onion, garlic, and green peppers in the olive oil until limp. Add to the sauce and cook for 5 minutes. Add the turkey meat, and heat through. Finally add the olives and blanched almonds, and cook for another 2 or 3 minutes. Serve with rice, polenta, or tortillas.

Serves eight to ten.

TURKEY DIVAN

Cover the bottom of a large, flat casserole with cooked (not over-cooked) broccoli. Arrange slices of cooked turkey on top and mask with mornay sauce (page 238). Sprinkle with grated Parmesan cheese and put under the broiler for a few minutes to glaze.

TURKEY MOLE

  1 turkey breast and wing
  1½ teaspoons salt
  2 medium onions, chopped
  Bacon fat or oil
  2 cloves garlic
  2 tablespoons chili powder
  1 small dried hot chili pepper
  1 cup ground almonds, walnuts, peanuts, or cashews
  2 ounces bitter chocolate
  1 cup ripe olives

➣ Cut the breast into four pieces and the wing into two. Place in a deep pot, add water to cover, and bring to a boil. Add the salt and simmer for 30 minutes.

Brown the onions in either bacon fat or oil, and add to the pot with the garlic, chili powder, hot chili pepper, ground nuts, and chocolate. Cover the pot and simmer until the sauce is thickened and the turkey is tender. Taste for salt. Ten minutes before serving, add the olives and heat through. Serve with polenta or tortillas.

Serves four.

CURRIED LEFTOVER TURKEY

1 large onion, chopped
2 tablespoons butter
1 apple, cored but not peeled, finely chopped
1 green pepper, seeded and finely chopped
2 tablespoons curry powder
2 cups turkey or chicken broth
Cooked turkey wings, disjointed
Meat from cooked turkey legs and thighs, cut into pieces
Leftover turkey gravy
Salt and freshly ground black pepper
½ cup seedless white grapes

Sauté the onion in the butter till soft. Add the apple and green pepper and cook till tender. Mix in the curry powder and cook for a few minutes to remove the raw taste. Pour in the broth and simmer for 10 minutes.

Add the turkey pieces and cook until they are heated through. Mix in any leftover turkey gravy. Season to taste and mix in the grapes. Serve with steamed rice, chutney, chopped salted peanuts, thinly sliced cucumbers dressed with oil and vinegar, and baked bananas. Beer is good with this.

TURKEY AND ALMOND CRÊPES

2½ cups diced cooked turkey

2 cups turkey broth

4 tablespoons butter

4 tablespoons flour

1 teaspoon dried tarragon

1 teaspoon salt

2 tablespoons bourbon

1 cup heavy cream

3 egg yolks

¾ cup toasted salted almonds

12 crêpes (see page 92)

¼ cup grated Parmesan cheese

Cover the turkey with ½ cup of broth, heat through, and keep warm. Melt the butter in a heavy saucepan, blend in the flour, and cook over low heat for a minute or so. Do not brown. Stir in the rest of the broth and continue to stir and cook until thickened. Add the tarragon, salt, and bourbon. Blend the cream and egg yolks, and stir in a few spoonfuls of the hot sauce, then gradually stir this back into the sauce, and continue to stir and cook over medium heat until thickened. Do not allow to boil.

Combine half the sauce with the turkey, in its broth, and the almonds. Spoon this mixture on the crêpes and roll them up. Arrange in a buttered baking dish. Add the Parmesan cheese to the remaining sauce and pour it over the crêpes. Bake in a 450°F oven until the sauce has delicately browned, or brown under the broiler.

Serves four.

GRILLED LEFTOVER TURKEY LEGS

Remove the legs from a roasted turkey. With a sharp knife, cut away the meat from the bone in one piece. Fill with leftover stuffing and tie securely. Dip in beaten egg, then in bread crumbs. Sauté in butter till nicely browned on all sides. Serve with tomato sauce.

TURKEY LOAF

2 cups cooked turkey pieces
1 cup stuffing
Salt and freshly ground black pepper
2 egg yolks
½ cup milk
1 cup béchamel sauce (page 237) or tomato sauce
1 tablespoon grated onion
2 tablespoons chopped parsley

Preheat the oven to 350°F.

Mince the turkey meat in a food processor or put through a grinder. Mix with the stuffing, and salt and pepper to taste. Beat the egg yolks well and add the milk. Mix with the turkey, and taste for seasoning. Place in a buttered loaf pan and bake in the preheated oven for 40 minutes.

Prepare a béchamel sauce or a tomato sauce, and season with the onion and parsley. Serve with the unmolded turkey loaf.

Serves four to six.

TURKEY HASH

5 tablespoons butter
½ cup finely chopped onion
2 cloves garlic, finely chopped
½ green pepper, seeded and finely chopped
3 cups diced, cooked turkey
1 cup cooked stuffing
Salt and freshly ground black pepper
⅔ cup pitted black olives
½ cup toasted almonds
½ cup heavy cream
Chopped parsley

Melt the butter in a heavy skillet over medium heat, and sauté the onion, garlic, and green pepper until limp and just delicately brown. Add the turkey and stuffing and toss well with the onion and green pepper. Add salt and pepper to taste. Allow the mixture to cook till thoroughly warmed through. Turn, and blend in the olives and almonds. Dribble the cream over all, and let the hash cook down till nicely crusty at the bottom and piping hot. Add the chopped parsley and invert onto a hot platter, or serve from the skillet in which it was made.

Serves six.

TURKEY SOUFFLÉ

4 tablespoons lard

3 tablespoons flour

1 cup turkey broth or milk

1 teaspoon salt

½ teaspoon freshly ground black pepper

⅛ teaspoon nutmeg

4 egg yolks, lightly beaten

1 cup ground cooked turkey

4 egg whites, beaten until stiff but not dry

For the béchamel sauce

3 tablespoons butter

2 tablespoons flour

1 cup turkey broth

½ cup light cream or half-and-half

½ teaspoon salt

¼ teaspoon freshly ground black pepper

Melt the lard in a heavy saucepan over medium heat, blend in the flour, and stir for about 2 minutes. Add the broth or milk, and continue to stir until thickened. Add the seasonings. Remove from the heat and allow to cool slightly.

Stir a couple of spoonfuls of the sauce into the beaten yolks, and blend this thoroughly with the remaining sauce. Mix in the turkey and then fold in the beaten egg whites. Pour into a buttered 1½-quart soufflé dish, and bake at 400°F for 25 to 35 minutes.

Make the béchamel sauce. Melt the butter in a small saucepan, blend in the flour, and stir over medium heat for about 2 minutes. Add the broth and stir until thickened. Then add the light cream or half-and-half and the salt and pepper, and stir until thickened again and smooth. Serve sauce over soufflé.

Serves four.

TURKEY TONNATO

1¼ cups homemade mayonnaise (page 240)
1 teaspoon very finely chopped onion
1 can (7 ounces) albacore or white-meat tuna, drained
2 anchovies, finely chopped
Cooked turkey breast, thinly sliced
Cherry tomatoes and black olives for garnish

❧ Prepare the mayonnaise and add the onion. Mix with the flaked tuna and anchovies. Marinate for several hours in the refrigerator to mellow the flavors. Arrange the turkey slices on a serving platter, mask with the tuna sauce, and garnish with cherry tomatoes and black olives.

TURKEY AND HAM IN ASPIC

2 cups shredded, cooked turkey
1 large slice baked ham or 2 large slices cooked tongue, shredded
1 tablespoon (1 envelope) unflavored gelatin
¼ cup cold water
2 cups boiling turkey or chicken broth
1 tablespoon lemon juice
2 teaspoons Worcestershire sauce
Salt and freshly ground black pepper
Stuffed olives, sliced
Hard-boiled eggs, sliced

❧ Combine the shredded meats and set aside. Prepare an aspic by dissolving the gelatin in the cold water, then adding the boiling turkey or chicken broth. Stir in the lemon juice, Worcestershire sauce, and salt and pepper to taste. Allow to cool.

Pour a thin layer of the aspic in a 6-cup ring mold and cool it until it is firm. Place a ring of sliced, stuffed olives and sliced hard-boiled eggs on the gelatin. Then add the shreds of turkey and ham or tongue. Pour the remaining aspic mixture over all and allow it to chill. Unmold on a large plate. Fill the center with either cole slaw or beet and egg salad, dressed with vinaigrette dressing.

Serves four.

TURKEY AND WALNUT SALAD

2 cups diced cooked turkey breast
1 cup toasted walnuts
½ cup finely chopped celery
Mayonnaise and sour cream mixed
Lettuce
Hard-boiled eggs
Black olives

❧ Combine the turkey, walnuts, and celery, and add enough mayonnaise and sour cream to bind well. Serve on lettuce leaves, and garnish with sliced hard-boiled eggs and olives.

Serves four.

CREAMED TURKEY AND TURKEY SALADS

For creamed turkey dishes and other turkey salads, follow the recipes given for chicken.

COLD TURKEY FOR BUFFETS

Turkey is an ideal buffet food, although it has been overworked in that role. Serve thinly sliced on a platter, garnished with fresh vegetables, olives, or pickles, or serve in combination with either sliced ham or sliced tongue, along with mustard, hot or sweet. Or prepare a wide assortment of turkey sandwiches, following the recipes for chicken given on pages 103–104. Turkey Tonnato (page 148) makes a nice change from the usual presentation.

SMOKED TURKEY

For Hors d'Oeuvre

Serve smoked turkey either hot or cold, carved from the bird as needed; or serve in any of the following ways:
1. Place thin slices of turkey on fingers of buttered pumpernickel or rye.
2. Combine strips of smoked turkey and Swiss cheese.
3. Spear cubes of turkey and avocado on small wooden skewers and dip in Russian dressing.
4. Mix cubes of turkey with chopped walnuts, celery, and mayonnaise, and serve on hot toast.

Other Uses

Serve sliced cold as a buffet dish along with a complementary meat like tongue or pork (never ham or beef).
1. Cut into julienne for a chef's salad or an avocado and grapefruit salad.
2. Dice and make into smoked turkey hash (see Turkey Hash, page 146).

North American Wild Turkey

The North American wild turkey is, as its name implies, truly American. It should be prepared with simplicity. To begin with, this bird differs from its domestic kin in shape, size, and flavor. It has an enormously deep breast and longer legs, and the dark meat is as epicurean as the light. Seldom exceeding 12 to 15 pounds for the toms, and 10 to 12 pounds for the hens, it is built for speed both in running and gliding to cover.

As for flavor, it differs as much from the domestic turkey as, for example, the mallard does from the Peking duck. It can not be said to have a gamy taste, as does the pheasant or quail. But the rich difference is there, and is greatly preferred to the flavor of domestic varieties. Contrary to most other game birds, the flesh is juicy, not dry.

The preparation is in principle similar to the roasting of any domestic bird. It should be stuffed with only the simplest ingredients: dry bread crumbs added to finely chopped onions, leeks, and celery, which have been lightly sautéed in butter. Mix all together until well blended, adding salt and pepper, and last the liver (gizzard, too, if you like it) which has been poached and chopped. Simmer the gizzard and the neck together with a little water to make a broth, and set aside for addition to the gravy after the bird is done.

Stuff the bird with this mixture, and do not worry if the dressing seems dry; it picks up plenty of moisture from the turkey while cooking, and a soggy dressing is insufferable. Roast until done in a 350°F oven, basting at least every 15 minutes. It needs no cover, or larding, but it must be basted constantly for a perfect glaze. Never add water to a roasting bird. When done remove the turkey to a hot platter and keep warm while making the gravy. Use the roasting pan and pour off excess fat, of which there should be plenty. Add the broth from the neck and gizzard, and be sure to dissolve the little brown pieces stuck to the pan; that is where the best flavor is. Add salt and freshly ground black pepper to taste. And just before serving, swirl a little butter in it, which thickens it just enough. Wild turkey needs no dressing up; it is quite good enough of itself to bring out its own flavor. Serve with boiled and well-buttered hominy or samp, and braised leeks, or the tenderest kale.

A fine California Cabernet or a good French Burgundy will complement this truly wonderful bird.

CHAPTER 3

Duck

੪

The duck commonly available in this country is the Long Island strain, developed with a heavy layer of fat, which produces a juicier, tenderer bird but gives relatively little meat for its size. Thus a duck of 4 to 5 pounds will feed only two people well. For the best results, the Long Island duck should be roasted in a moderate oven for sufficient time to allow the fat to render. The skin can be crisped by roasting at high heat for the final period of cooking.

Most Long Island ducks are sold frozen and should be thawed before cooking. This will take 1 to 1½ days in the refrigerator, 4 to 5 hours at room temperature, or 2 to 3 hours in cool water.

Fresh-killed ducks can often be found in Chinese markets, with head and feet intact, and sometimes in country markets. In Pennsylvania one finds Muscovy duck, which is a leaner but tougher bird than the Long Island and is best when braised. Generally, most of the population will encounter nothing during their lifetime except frozen Long Island duckling.

ROAST DUCKLING

1 duck, 4 to 5 pounds
Salt and freshly ground black pepper
Dried thyme or rosemary
1 onion, stuck with 2 cloves

🦆 Preheat the oven to 350°F.

Rub the duckling with salt and pepper and thyme or rosemary. Place the onion in the cavity. Set the duckling on a rack in a roasting pan. Roast in the preheated oven, allowing 1 hour for rare duck, 1½ hours for medium rare, and 2 hours for well done. After 30 minutes of roasting, prick the skin all over several times to release the fat. If you like a crisp skin, increase the heat to 500°F for the final 15 minutes of roasting and cut the total roasting time by 5 minutes.

To test for doneness, prick the thigh joint with a fork. If the juices run pink, the duck should be medium rare; if they run clear, it should be well done.

Duck does not lend itself to carving, and it is best to cut it into halves or quarters with poultry shears.

One duckling will feed two people.

Variations

1. *With curry and honey:* Mix ¼ cup honey with 1½ tablespoons curry powder. After the duck has cooked for 1 hour, brush at intervals with this mixture to give the skin a nice glaze.
2. *Au poivre:* Half an hour before the duck is done, remove it from the oven and press 1 tablespoon coarsely ground black pepper into the skin. Return to the oven to finish roasting.

ROAST DUCK WITH ORANGES

1 clove garlic
2 oranges, peeled and separated into sections
1 duck, 4 to 5 pounds
Salt and freshly ground black pepper
1 cup orange juice
1 tablespoon grated orange zest
¼ cup orange liqueur
1½ teaspoons butter

Preheat the oven to 350°F.

Insert the garlic and orange sections in the cavity of the duck. Rub the skin with salt and pepper. Place on a rack in a roasting pan and roast as directed in the preceding recipe, basting several times with orange juice. When the bird is done, transfer to a warm platter while you prepare the sauce.

Skim the excess fat from the roasting pan and add the orange zest, remaining orange juice, and orange liqueur. Reduce the sauce over high heat until it has thickened slightly. Add salt and pepper to taste and swirl in the butter. Cut the duck into quarters and serve with the oranges and sauce.

Serves two.

ROAST DUCK WITH SAUERKRAUT

½ cup finely diced salt pork
1 medium onion, finely chopped
1 apple, finely chopped
Salt and freshly ground black pepper to taste
1 sprig thyme
Caraway seeds
2 pounds sauerkraut
2 ducks, 5 pounds each
White wine

Preheat the oven to 350°F.

Render the salt pork in a skillet. Add the onion and apple and sauté gently, then add salt and pepper. Add the thyme and a few caraway seeds, then add the sauerkraut. Mix well and stuff the ducks with the mixture. Sew up the vents.

Place the ducks, breast side up, on a trivet in a roasting pan. Place in the preheated oven and roast according to the directions on page 154, basting with wine several times. Remove the ducks to a hot platter. Skim the excess fat from the pan and let the sauce cook down for 3 minutes. Pour around the ducks and serve with a potato purée.

Serves four.

DUCK WITH OLIVES

2 ducks, 5 pounds each, necks and giblets reserved
1 onion, stuck with 2 cloves
2 carrots
1 bay leaf
Salt and freshly ground black pepper
Sprigs of parsley
10 to 12 cloves garlic
1½ cups small unpitted green olives
Beurre manié (a little flour and butter kneaded together)

Prepare 2 cups broth by simmering for 1 hour, in water to cover, the neck and giblets of the duck, the onion stuck with the cloves, the carrots, bay leaf, and salt and pepper to taste.

Preheat the oven to 350°F.

Rub the ducks with a damp cloth. Place several sprigs of parsley and 5 or 6 garlic cloves in the cavity of each duck, then place on a trivet in a shallow pan. Roast in the preheated oven, allowing 18 to 20 minutes per pound. After 30 minutes, prick the skin all over; baste once or twice with broth. Thirty minutes before the ducks are done, increase the temperature to 450°F to crisp the skin. Twenty minutes later, add the green olives. When the ducks are tender, season with salt and pepper to taste and remove to a hot platter. Skim the excess fat from the pan and add the remaining broth. Reduce over high heat, and thicken with beurre manié added in small bits, and salt and pepper to taste. Pour the sauce with the olives around the ducks.

Serves four.

CASSEROLE OF DUCK WITH YOGURT

2 ducks, 5 pounds each, giblets reserved and chopped

Flour for dredging

¼ cup oil or 4 tablespoons butter

Salt and freshly ground black pepper to taste

2 medium onions, finely chopped

3 tablespoons chopped parsley

Pinch of dried rosemary

Pinch of dried thyme

1 clove garlic, peeled

2 cups white wine

1 cup yogurt

🌰 Preheat the oven to 350°F.

Cut up the ducks into convenient serving pieces (carving shears are a great help here). Prick the skin well. Dredge the pieces with flour and sear them well in oil or butter. Drain on paper towels and transfer to an ovenproof casserole. Season with salt and pepper to taste. Add the chopped giblets, onion, parsley, rosemary, thyme, and garlic. Pour in the white wine and cover the casserole. Place in the preheated oven and cook for 1½ hours. Test for tenderness. If necessary, continue cooking until done, about 30 minutes more. Remove the ducks to a hot platter. Skim off excess fat from the pan juices, add the yogurt, and heat through; do not allow to boil. Correct the seasoning. Serve with rice and buttered turnips.

Serves four to six.

CASSEROLE OF DUCK WITH RED CABBAGE

2 ducks, 5 pounds each

Flour for dredging

Salt and freshly ground black pepper

6 tablespoons cooking oil or butter

1 onion, finely chopped

Caraway seeds

Pinch of dried sweet basil

1 medium head red cabbage, shredded

3 tablespoons wine vinegar

2 tablespoons brown sugar

~❧ Preheat the oven to 350°F.

Skin and cut up the ducks into convenient serving pieces. Dredge with flour, salt, and pepper. Brown in ¼ cup oil or 4 tablespoons butter, drain on paper towels, and transfer the pieces to an oven-proof casserole. Add the onion, a few caraway seeds, and sweet basil, and bake in the preheated oven for 30 minutes.

While the ducks are cooking, heat the remaining oil or butter in the skillet in which you browned the ducks and add the red cabbage. Cook down quickly for 10 minutes, tossing it well. Add the wine vinegar, brown sugar, and salt and pepper to taste. Simmer for 5 minutes. Add to the casserole, cover, and simmer till the ducks are tender, about 1 hour more. Serve with potato pancakes.

Serves four to six.

CASSEROLE OF DUCK WITH PINTO BEANS

2 cups dried pinto beans
2 cloves garlic
1 bay leaf
1 onion, stuck with 2 cloves
2 ducks, 5 pounds each
Flour for dredging
Salt and freshly ground black pepper
2 tablespoons butter
3 slices salt pork, diced
2 medium onions, finely chopped
Pinch of dried sweet basil
½ teaspoon dry mustard

Soak the pinto beans overnight (or follow directions on the package). Drain, then add the garlic, bay leaf, and onion. Cover with boiling, salted water and cook until tender. Drain, reserving the liquid.

Preheat the oven to 350°F.

Skin and cut up the ducks in convenient serving pieces. Cut the skin in thin strips and set aside. Dredge the ducks in flour seasoned with salt and pepper. Melt the butter in a skillet and render the salt pork. Add the chopped onions and sauté till limp. Transfer the pieces of salt pork and the onions to a casserole. Sear the ducks in the salt pork fat and also transfer to the casserole.

Add the beans, sweet basil, freshly ground black pepper, and dry mustard. Mix the duck with the beans. Pour in enough bean liquid to cover and let simmer, covered, in the preheated oven, till the beans and ducks are thoroughly tender, about 2 hours. Add more liquid if it cooks away too quickly.

Deep-fry the strips of skin in oil heated to 355°F for 2 to 3 minutes to crisp. Drain. Use as garnish for the ducks.

Serves six.

DUCK WITH WHITE WINE

2 ducks, 4 to 5 pounds each

Coarse salt

½ teaspoon ground ginger

¼ teaspoon ground cloves

⅓ cup Cognac

2 cups light dry wine

2 small onions, each stuck with a clove

2 small carrots

⅔ cup white raisins

2 tablespoons beurre manié (butter and flour, kneaded together)

Rub the duck cavities and skin with a mixture of salt, ginger, and cloves. Truss and place on a rack in a roasting pan. Roast at 350°F for 1 hour. Transfer to a deep braising pan, but leave the oven on. Warm the Cognac and carefully flame the ducks. Then add the wine and vegetables. Place in the oven, and cook another 30 to 45 minutes, basting the ducks with the pan liquid several times. Remove the ducks, and strain the sauce. Discard the vegetables. Return the ducks to the pan with the sauce, and add the raisins. Cook for 10 to 15 minutes more, basting once. Transfer the ducks to a hot serving platter. Cut into halves or quarters with poultry shears. Skim of excess fat from the sauce and thicken the sauce with the beurre manié. Pour some sauce around the ducks and pass the rest separately.

Serves 4.

BRAISED DUCK WITH PORT

1 duck, 5 pounds
Stuffing of your choice (see pages 227–236)
¼ cup cooking oil or 4 tablespoons butter
2 slices lemon
1 cup port, more as needed
2 tablespoons grated orange zest
1 teaspoon lemon juice
Salt and freshly ground black pepper to taste

Preheat the oven to 350°F.

Stuff the duck, and sew up or skewer the vent. Brown in the oil or butter. Transfer to an ovenproof casserole and add lemon slices and port. Cover and braise in the preheated oven for 2 hours, basting with additional wine three or four times during the cooking. Prick the skin with a fork to release the fat. When the duck has achieved the proper degree of tenderness, remove it to a hot platter and skim all excess fat from the casserole. Add the orange zest and lemon juice and reduce the sauce. Correct the seasoning and pour around the duck. Serve with wild rice.

Serves two.

BROILED DUCKLING

Split a 4- to 5-pound duck down the back or have the butcher do it for you. Wash and thoroughly dry, then place, skin side down, in a preheated 350°F broiler 6 inches from the heat. Broil for 18 minutes. Turn, prick the skin, and continue broiling for 15 to 18 minutes, watching carefully. Salt and pepper well on each side. Serve with wild rice, green salad, and a good Beaujolais.

Serves two.

PHILIP BROWN'S DUCK KEBABS

2 ducks, 4 to 5 pounds each
½ cup olive oil
½ cup orange juice
1 tablespoon grated orange zest
4 tablespoons grated onion
1 garlic clove, crushed
6 oranges
Pitted green olives
Salt and freshly ground black pepper

Cut off the breast and thigh meat from the ducks, leaving the skin intact, and then slice into strips about 2 inches by 1 inch. In a large bowl, combine the olive oil, orange juice, orange zest, grated onion and garlic. Add the duck pieces, and marinate for 2 hours.

Blanch the whole oranges in boiling water for 3 minutes and drain. Leave unpeeled, and cut in wedges about an inch wide. Thread the duck and orange wedges on skewers, along with a few green olives. Season with salt and pepper. Broil about 4 inches from the heating unit, skin side up, for 10 minutes. Turn and broil for another 5 minutes. This should yield pinkish meat and a crisp skin. Serve with a risotto or buttered noodles.

Serves six.

BROILED DUCKLING AU POIVRE

1 duck, 4 to 5 pounds, split in half, wings removed
½ lemon
1 teaspoon salt
1 tablespoon crushed black peppercorns

🦆 Rub the bone side of the duck with half a lemon, and sprinkle the skin side with salt. Arrange, bone side up, on a rack in a broiling pan. Broil 6 inches from the heating unit for 20 minutes. Turn, prick the surface of the skin well with a fork, and continue broiling for 10 minutes. Remove and press the skin side of each half into the crushed peppercorns, using wadded paper towels to protect your hands. Broil, skin side up, for another 10 to 15 minutes, or until browned and crisp.

Serves two.

COLD DUCK WITH MAYONNAISE

2 ducks, 5 pounds each
2 onions, each stuck with 1 or 2 cloves
4 carrots
1 bay leaf
3 to 4 stalks celery
Bouquet garni (1 sprig thyme, 1 sprig parsley, few leaves tarragon and
*   rosemary, and a few juniper berries, tied in cheesecloth)*
Salt and freshly ground black pepper
Cold water to cover
Romaine leaves
Homemade mayonnaise (page 240)
Garnishes (see page 165)

Place the ducks in a deep kettle with the onions, carrots, bay leaf, celery, bouquet garni, and salt and pepper to taste. Cover with cold water, bring to a boil, then reduce the heat and simmer till the ducks are tender, about 1½ hours. Remove from the broth and cool. Save the broth for soups or for aspic jelly (see below).

Skin the ducks and cut into convenient serving pieces, removing the bones. Arrange on a chilled platter nicely covered with leaves of romaine. Spoon the mayonnaise over the duck. Garnish with capers, chopped parsley, tomato quarters, hard-boiled eggs, and pimiento strips. Serve with more mayonnaise.

Serves six.

Variation

Duck in Aspic: Strain 4 cups of the degreased broth through cheese-cloth, return it to a small saucepan, and add the beaten white of an egg and the shell. Bring to a boil; strain again.

Melt 2 tablespoons (2 envelopes) unflavored gelatin in ½ cup cold water. Add to the boiling broth and stir till the gelatin is thoroughly blended. Add 1 tablespoon lemon juice and a few grains of cayenne. Cool until almost jellied. Dip each piece of duck in the jelly and set aside to chill. Arrange on a platter and garnish with mayonnaise and tomatoes and cucumber. Chop the remaining jelly in small cubes and arrange around the platter. If you like, cut the skin into strips, deep-fry (see page 160), and use as a garnish. Serve with a green salad.

DUCK AND ORANGE SALAD

2 cups cooked duck breast meat, diced

2 medium oranges, peeled and cut into sections

1 large red onion, sliced thin and broken into rings

1 cup celery root, peeled and cut into julienne

Romaine lettuce leaves

Mayonnaise, preferably homemade, flavored with lemon juice to taste

 Toss the duck, orange sections, and vegetables together. Arrange romaine leaves in a bowl or serving dish and add the duck mixture. Pass the mayonnaise separately.

Serves four.

Wild Duck

No two people seem to agree upon the proper length of time to cook a wild duck. There is the cook-till-the-flesh-falls-off-the-bones school; and those happy in-betweens who just like to eat wild duck because it sounds nice. I like mine rare with some blood running.

Over a hundred varieties of wild duck are known, but the choice we are usually given is rather limited. The most common are the mallard, the canvasback, the teal—all excellent in their ways. The teal is quite small—in fact some of my friends have been known to eat two and even three at a meal.

Wild ducks are sometimes hell to pick. They are more often than not covered with pin feathers that stick like glue. Singe the birds well, sit down with a pair of tweezers, and do the best you can. Draw the wild duck as you would any other bird, taking special caution not to break the gall bladder.

If you are of the long-cooking school, you will want a savory stuffing for your birds. Choose any stuffing you like, although I have given a simple stuffing (page 233) that goes admirably with duck.

One half-duck usually constitutes a serving unless the birds are very small, when a whole one, or possibly two, is the required portion. Carving shears are a must with all kinds of game birds.

Wild ducks can be roasted or braised in the manner of domestic ducks, if you so desire (see pages 153–162), but they will not be as satisfactory.

Wild rice or fried hominy, turnips, and green peas are traditional accompaniments. Some people insist on a tart jelly. I hate it. I'd much rather have a mellow, well-rounded wine to enhance the flavor of the duck, such as a California Cabernet or a fine French Burgundy.

Leftover wild duck may be made into a salmi or used as you would domestic duck. It is delicious cold with a salad.

ROAST WILD DUCK I

Singe, pick, and clean the ducks. Insert a sprig of parsley or a few juniper berries in the vent of each, if you like. Place on a rack in a shallow roasting pan and rub the breasts with butter. For blood-rare, roast in a preheated 475° to 500°F oven 15 to 20 minutes, depending upon the size of the ducks. Baste every 5 minutes with melted butter or a mixture of melted butter and red wine. Season with salt and pepper to taste and remove to a hot platter. These birds will give plenty of rich, red juices when a sharp knife is sunk into the breasts.

ROAST WILD DUCK II

Singe and clean each duck, and stuff it if you wish. (Do not use a stuffing containing pork unless previously cooked.) Close the vent and tie a piece of larding pork around the breast. Place on a rack in a roasting pan, breast side up, and roast in a preheated 350°F oven, allowing 15 minutes to the pound. Baste with melted butter or red wine. Many people prefer to cover the ducks when roasting this way, but I do not advise it.

BROILED WILD DUCK

Small young ducks may be broiled either split or whole. Rub well with butter or oil and place on a rack in a preheated broiler, skin side down, if split; on one side, if whole. Broil for 10 to 20 minutes, depending upon how well done you like your duck. Turn frequently, especially if you are broiling a whole bird.

OREGON WILD DUCK

Stuff a duck with pieces of onion, celery, and apple. Close the vent with a piece of foil. Salt and pepper the breast and lay a piece of bacon across it. Roast on a rack in a roasting pan in a hot (400°F) oven, 45 minutes for a large duck and less time for teal or small ducks. Baste occasionally with red wine. This results in a juicy but not bloody bird.

Traditionally this duck was served with elderberry jelly and wild rice. The rice is excellent with a duck gravy made thus:

1 onion, finely chopped
Gizzard and heart of the duck, chopped
3 tablespoons butter
2 cups boiling water
Pan drippings
Beurre manié (a little flour and butter kneaded together)
Freshly ground black pepper
Pinch of cayenne
¼ cup Cognac

Sauté the onion with the chopped heart and gizzard in the butter. Add the boiling water and simmer for perhaps an hour. Add the pan drippings from the roast duck and thicken with the beurre manié, added in bits. Season highly with pepper, and add cayenne and Cognac.

MARY FROST MABON'S ST. LOUIS WILD DUCKS

Mary Frost Mabon, who used to write for *Harper's Bazaar* as their food and wine editor and wrote several cookbooks, was a great fancier of good food. Here is her version of an old family recipe:

"These ducks are cooked on the top of the stove in a thin aluminum pan, of a size to hold two ducks. First make as hot a fire as your stove will give. Then melt enough fat (one-half lard, one-half butter) in your pan to half cover your birds. When this boils in the pan over the very hot fire put in the ducks breast-side down, cover with a lid (but see to it this is so placed that steam can escape).

Leave this for 7 minutes, then remove the lid and turn the birds over. After they are turned pour 2 tablespoons of Italian vermouth over the breasts, then put the lid on and allow to cook for another 7 minutes. Take off the lid again, turn the ducks over on their breasts again, pour a little vermouth over their backs and let them stay there 2 minutes.

"Now turn the birds again and test with a fork. If blood comes out, they must be turned again for 2 minutes. If a clear liquid comes out they are done. Remove the birds to a warm pan while you cool the contents left in the aluminum pan quickly by setting it in a dishpan filled with ice and water. The fat can then be rapidly poured off, or removed from the top. The juice will be left; add to it previously prepared sliced orange peel with salt, pepper, paprika, 2 tablespoons of vermouth and as much currant jelly as you fancy. Heat, pour over your birds on a deep platter and bear triumphantly to the carver."

Note: Quail can be cooked the same way in a smaller pan, with 1½ minute turnings.

WILD DUCK IN THE MUD

If you just can't wait till you return to civilization, choose a young duck from your catch, remove the head, slit the vent, and draw the entrails. Wash thoroughly. Salt and pepper the cavity and in it place an apple or an onion. Roll the whole thing, feathers and all, in thick, gooey (but clean-smelling) mud or clay. It should be caked on thickly to make it airtight. Place in hot coals or on a grill over a brisk fire until the mud or clay dries out. Split the coating and remove; the feathers will come along with it. Add a little butter and salt and pepper, and eat away.

✢ CHAPTER 4 ✢
Squab and Pigeon

❧

Squab and pigeon appear in our markets in more or less limited quantities, but their distinctive flavor makes them well worth considering as a change from the other poultry and game birds. They weigh from ¾ pound to 1¼ pounds and are served either whole or split and butterflied, usually one to a person. They can be roasted, broiled, or sautéed and generally call for eating with the fingers.

ROAST SQUAB
Stuff the squab, if you wish (see pages 227–236), and butter well or cover the breast with bacon. Roast on a rack in a preheated 400°F oven from 30 to 40 minutes, or until tender. Test by pricking the thigh joint to see if the juices run clear. The birds should be rather well done. Season with salt and pepper to taste. Serve on well-browned fried hominy squares.

STUFFED SQUAB

8 squab, with giblets

12 shallots, finely chopped

4 tablespoons butter

½ plus ⅓ cup Cognac

2 cloves garlic

1 pound ground pork

½ pound ground veal

1 cup fresh bread crumbs

2 truffles, finely chopped

½ cup finely chopped parsley

1 teaspoon dried thyme or dried rosemary

1½ teaspoons salt

½ teaspoon Quatre Épices (see page 173) or a tiny pinch each of white
  pepper, nutmeg, ginger, and cloves

Salt and freshly ground black pepper

2 eggs

8 strips bacon

Watercress for garnish

1½ cups Quick Brown Sauce (see page 173)

Gently sauté the giblets and chopped shallots in the butter for 3 to 4 minutes. Blend in a food processor or electric blender with the ½ cup of Cognac and the garlic. Mix with the ground meats, bread crumbs, truffles, herbs, seasonings, and eggs. Stuff the squab with this mixture, and truss them (see page 57). Arrange breast side up on a rack in a baking pan or dish, and drape a strip of bacon over each breast. Roast for 15 minutes at 450°F, then reduce the heat to 350°F and roast 30 to 40 minutes longer, basting with the pan drippings.

When the squab are done, remove the rack from the roasting pan, pour out any drippings, and reserve. Replace the squab in the pan, pour the remaining Cognac over them, and flame them—be careful of a sudden flare-up. Transfer the squab to a platter, and garnish with watercress.

To serve with a brown sauce, remove excess fat from the pan juices, combine the juices with the brown sauce (see below), and heat through. Serve separately.

Serves eight.

Quatre Épices

1⅛ cups ground white pepper
3½ tablespoons ground nutmeg
3½ tablespoons ground ginger
1½ tablespoons ground cloves

🍃 Blend these four spices well, and store in a tightly sealed jar, to be used as needed.

Quick Brown Sauce

6 tablespoons unsalted butter
3 shallots, finely chopped
1 cup dry red wine
1 can (10½ ounces) beef bouillon
Pinch of dried thyme
3 tablespoons flour
Salt and freshly ground black pepper

🍃 Melt 3 tablespoons of butter in a heavy saucepan and sauté the shallots over medium heat until wilted. Add the wine, bouillon, and thyme. Bring to a boil and continue to cook over high heat until reduced by half. Meanwhile, work the remaining butter and flour into a paste and roll into tiny balls (beurre manié). Drop a couple at a time into the boiling liquid and stir until they are completely absorbed before adding more. Continue cooking and stirring until the sauce is thickened. Season to taste with salt and pepper. Put through a strainer to remove the shallots and any lumps.

Makes 1½ cups.

BROILED SQUAB

Split the squab down the back and flatten it out. Rub well with butter or other fat, place on a rack, and broil for 15 minutes, turning once. Season with salt and pepper to taste.

Squab may be broiled whole, but they must be turned often to get an even color on all sides. Give them 20 minutes. Serve one to a person. You'll have to use your fingers to nibble bits from the bone.

BROILED SQUAB WITH ROSEMARY BUTTER

Follow the recipe for broiled chicken with rosemary butter (page 48). Remove the backbone and flatten the squab. Broil bone side up for 8 minutes, then turn and broil for another 6 minutes.

SQUAB SAUTÉ WITH BACON

1 squab, split and flattened
Salt and freshly ground black pepper
6 to 8 slices bacon
Chopped parsley

🐦 Salt and pepper the squab. Sauté the bacon slices in a skillet till crisp. Remove the bacon and keep hot. Gently sauté the squab in the bacon fat for 15 to 20 minutes, or until the bird is tender. Sprinkle with chopped parsley and serve with the crisp bacon slices.

Serves one.

SQUAB SAUTÉ WITH WHITE WINE AND HERBS

8 tablespoons butter or butter and oil
4 small squab, split down the back and flattened
Salt and freshly ground black pepper
¼ cup chopped shallots
1½ cups white wine

¼ cup chopped parsley

2 tablespoons fresh tarragon or 2 teaspoons dried

4 slices crisp buttered toast

❧ Heat 4 tablespoons butter or butter and oil in each of two skillets and brown the squab halves on both sides over a brisk flame. Add salt and pepper to taste. To each skillet add half the chopped shallots and ½ cup white wine. Reduce the heat and cover the pans. Simmer for 15 minutes. Add 2 tablespoons chopped parsley and 1 tablespoon fresh tarragon or 1 teaspoon dried to each pan. Add a little more wine—about ½ cup altogether—and cook, uncovered, for 5 minutes. Serve on crisp buttered toast with the sauce spooned over.

Serves four.

SQUAB SAUTÉ WITH CABBAGE AND YOGURT

8 tablespoons butter or other fat

4 small squab, split down the back and flattened

Salt and freshly ground black pepper

1 small head cabbage, very finely shredded

1 cup yogurt

Chopped parsley

❧ Heat 4 tablespoons of butter in each of two skillets and brown the squab on both sides, then reduce the heat and sauté till tender, about 18 to 20 minutes, turning twice. Add salt and pepper to taste. Four to 8 minutes before the squab is done, cook the cabbage in boiling salted water until tender. Drain, add salt to taste and the yogurt, and mix well. Arrange on a large platter and place the squab halves on it. Sprinkle with chopped parsley and serve.

Serves four.

CASSEROLE OF SQUAB WITH TOMATOES

1 can (28 ounces) Italian plum tomatoes
5 small onions
6 tablespoons butter
Salt and freshly ground black pepper
4 squab
Parsley
6 slices bacon, diced
1 clove garlic, finely chopped
1 medium onion, very finely chopped
Pinch of dried thyme
Pinch of dried sweet basil
1 cup sliced mushrooms

🐦 Prepare a tomato sauce by putting the plum tomatoes through a food mill and reducing over medium heat with 1 small chopped onion until thickened. Stir in the butter, and add salt and pepper to taste. You should have about 2 cups of sauce.

Preheat the oven to 350°F.

Stuff each squab with a small onion and several sprigs of parsley. Sauté the bacon in a skillet. Remove the bacon and brown the squab in the fat very quickly, along with the garlic. Place the birds in a deep ovenproof casserole with the finely chopped onion, thyme, basil, mushrooms, and tomato sauce. Cover the casserole and simmer in the preheated oven for 1 hour, or until the birds are tender. Taste the sauce for seasoning. Serve with buttered noodles sprinkled with grated Parmesan cheese.

Serves four.

CASSEROLE OF PIGEON WITH RICE

4 young pigeons
¾ cup olive oil
Salt and freshly ground black pepper
2 onions, finely chopped
2 cloves garlic, finely chopped
1 green pepper, seeded and cut in thin strips
Chicken broth, heated
1½ cups raw rice
½ cup pine nuts
½ cup sliced mushrooms
3 pimientos, cut in thin strips

❧ Preheat the oven to 350°F.

Singe, draw, and clean the pigeons. Leave whole, or split, if you prefer. Heat ½ cup olive oil in a flameproof casserole and brown the pigeons well on all sides. Season with salt and pepper to taste, then add the onions, garlic, green pepper, and chicken broth. Cover the casserole and simmer in the preheated oven for 20 minutes—1 hour, for older pigeons.

Brown the raw rice very lightly in the remaining ¼ cup oil. Add to the casserole, along with the pine nuts, sliced mushrooms, and pimientos. Cover the whole with hot chicken broth. Replace in the oven, uncovered, and cook until the rice is tender and the broth is entirely cooked away. More broth may be added, if necessary.

Serves four to six.

CASSEROLE OF WOOD PIGEON WITH SAUERKRAUT

Wood pigeon, which used to be bountiful in the markets, is seldom found nowadays. However, people do shoot them in season and find them somewhat less tender than squab. Therefore they require longer, slower cooking.

4 wood pigeons
5 tablespoons bacon fat
Salt and freshly ground black pepper to taste
1 teaspoon dried thyme
½ teaspoon dried marjoram
1½ cups dry white wine
2 pounds sauerkraut
4 tart apples, peeled and quartered
1 teaspoon caraway seeds

❧ Preheat the oven to 350°F.

Singe, draw, and clean the wood pigeons. Melt the bacon fat in a flameproof casserole and brown the pigeons well on all sides over brisk heat. Add salt and pepper and the thyme, marjoram, and ½ cup wine. Cover the casserole and simmer in the preheated oven for 1 hour.

Drain the sauerkraut. Place it in a kettle with the apples, caraway seeds, and remaining white wine. Simmer over a low flame for 1 hour.

Remove the casserole from the oven. Arrange the sauerkraut around the birds. Cover the casserole and replace in the oven for 1 hour more, or until the pigeons are tender. Add more wine if the dish becomes too dry. Serve with mashed potatoes and more of the white wine, well chilled.

Serves four.

PIGEONS IN JELLY, A BEAUTIFUL DISH

Here is an eighteenth-century recipe for pigeon that I consider one of the most amusing I have ever encountered. Don't try it unless you have infinite patience and great feeling for the surrealist school of cookery.

"Pick two very nice pigeons, and make them look as well as possible by singeing, washing, and cleaning the heads well. Leave the heads and the feet on, but clip the nails close to the claws. Roast them of a very nice brown; and when done put a little sprig of myrtle into the bill of each. Have ready a savoury jelly, and with it half fill a bowl that is of a proper size to turn down on the dish you mean it to be served in. When the jelly and the birds are cold, see that no gravy hangs to the birds, and then lay them upside down in the jelly. Before the rest of it begins to set, pour it over the birds, so as to be three inches above the feet. This should be done full twenty-four hours before serving.

"This dish has a very handsome appearance in the middle range of a second course; or when served with the jelly roughed large, it makes a side or corner dish, its size being then less. The head should be kept up as if alive, by tying the neck with some thread, and the legs bent as if the pigeon sat upon them."

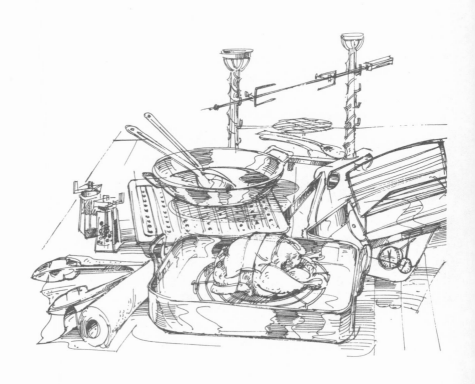

✦ CHAPTER 5 ✦

Goose

໒ຊ

Goose has never had great popularity in the United States. Although certain national groups have appreciated goose for generations, the average cook never dreams of buying one except for specific occasions. Even on holidays it is overlooked. The Thanksgiving and Christmas bird is invariably turkey, not goose. Yet since ancient times it has been much prized in Europe, especially in England, Germany, and France. It has been neglected here for perhaps two reasons: it is not a very economical bird, for there is a great deal of fat and a complex bone structure; and birds of good quality have not been generally available. However, an extremely fine goose has now been developed by the National Goose Council. Raised for tenderness and flavor, these are sold quick-frozen throughout the country. Weighing from 6 to 14 pounds, they come small enough to fit in anyone's oven.

Frozen goose must be thawed before cooking. There are three recommended ways to do this:

1. Leave the goose in its wrapping, place on a tray, and leave in the refrigerator—1 to 1½ days for a 6- to 10-pound bird; about 2 days for a 14-pound bird.

2. Leave the goose in its wrapping and immerse in cold water, changing the water often. Depending on the size of the goose, thawing will take 4 to 6 hours.

3. Leave the goose in its wrapping, set on a tray, and thaw at room temperature, which will take 6 to 12 hours.

Goose can be prepared much the same as domestic duck and should have a tart, savory stuffing. Sage is used for goose by many people, but I feel that this herb overpowers most poultry and advise against it. Apples and chestnuts and prunes are welcome ingredients in a goose stuffing (see page 234). Also consider the sauerkraut stuffing on page 234. If you use bread crumbs, be certain that the stuffing is dry, for the goose is fat and juicy and lubricates the cavity as it cooks.

ROAST GOOSE

Remove excess fat from the cavity of an 8- to 10-pound goose. Stuff with any of the stuffings suggested for goose (see pages 230–235), using ¾ to 1 cup per pound of bird. Truss, and sew up or skewer the vent. Rub with salt, and place, breast side up, on a rack in a roasting pan. Roast for 1 hour at 400°F in a preheated oven, then prick the skin all over to let the fat drain off. Reduce the temperature to 350°F and continue roasting until done, about another 1 to 1¾ hours. Remove the fat from the roasting pan as it accumulates, using a bulb baster or spoon, and reserve; it is an excellent fat for cooking. To test for doneness, prick the thigh joint with a fork. The juices should be clear, with perhaps a tinge of pink. Remove to a hot platter and allow to rest for 15 minutes before carving. Serve with the sauce for roast goose (page 184).

To Roast In A Microwave

Cover the legs and wings of the goose with small pieces of foil. (This will not affect the oven, due to the bird's large size.) Place the bird, breast side down, on inverted saucers in a 2-quart baking dish, thus holding the goose above and out of the juices. Cook, uncovered, for 30 minutes. Drain off juices and fat. Turn the goose breast side up and remove the foil. Continue cooking for an additional 30 minutes, or until a meat thermometer registers 180°F when inserted in the thigh. Remove from the oven, cover with foil, and let stand for about 10 to 15 minutes to allow the goose to finish cooking.

GOOSE BROTH

While the goose is roasting, prepare a stock for gravy or sauce.

Giblets and neck of the goose
1 or 2 sprigs parsley
1 onion, stuck with 1 clove
1 carrot, scraped
3 or 4 peppercorns
1 teaspoon salt
Cold water to cover

❦ Combine all the ingredients in a saucepan. Bring to a boil and skim, then reduce the heat and simmer, covered, for 1 hour.

Makes about 2 cups.

GOOSE GRAVY

¼ cup rendered goose fat

2 tablespoons flour

2 cups goose broth (see page 183), heated

Goose liver, sautéed in goose fat and chopped

Salt and freshly ground black pepper

🐦 Melt the goose fat in a saucepan. Stir in the flour and blend over low heat for 2 or 3 minutes. Add the broth, increase the heat, and stir until smooth and thickened. Add the chopped liver and salt and pepper to taste, and let simmer for several minutes more.

Makes about 2½ cups.

SAUCE FOR ROAST GOOSE

3 tablespoons rendered goose fat

1 medium onion, finely chopped

Goose liver, chopped

2 tablespoons chopped parsley

½ cup chopped mushrooms

1 cup goose broth (see page 183)

1 cup cream, blended with 2 egg yolks

2 tablespoons brandy

Salt and freshly ground black pepper

🐦 Melt the goose fat in a saucepan over medium heat. Sauté the onion until limp. Add the liver, parsley, and mushrooms; sauté for 5 minutes. Add the broth and simmer for 3 or 4 minutes. Finally add the cream mixed with the egg yolks. Stir constantly over low heat till the mixture thickens (do not allow to boil), and add the brandy. Season to taste.

Makes about 3 cups.

GOLDEN STATE GOOSE

1 goose, 8 to 10 pounds

4 shallots, chopped

3 tablespoons rendered goose fat

2 cups fresh bread crumbs

2 tablespoons chopped parsley

Pinch of dried thyme

1 tablespoon plus 1 teaspoon grated orange zest

1 cup almonds or walnuts, toasted

Goose liver, chopped

½ cup plus 3 tablespoons sherry

2 oranges, unpeeled and stuck with 3 cloves

Orange juice as needed

1 cup goose broth (see page 183)

*Beurre manié (1 tablespoon flour and 1 tablespoon butter kneaded
together)*

Salt and freshly ground black pepper

Preheat the oven to 400°F.

Stuff the goose with a stuffing made as follows: Sauté the shallots in the fat; add the bread crumbs, parsley, thyme, 1 tablespoon grated orange zest, nut meats, the chopped goose liver, and ½ cup sherry and mix well. Truss the goose (see page 125) and place on a rack in a roasting pan in which you have placed the oranges stuck with the cloves. Roast according to the directions on page 182, basting two or three times with orange juice.

Remove the goose to a hot platter. Discard the oranges. Skim the fat from the pan juices and add the broth. Set over low heat and stir in the beurre manié till well mixed and thickened. Add salt and pepper to taste, then add the remaining orange zest and sherry. Carve the goose and serve with the sauce.

Serves eight.

GOOSE ALSATIAN STYLE

1 medium onion, sliced

2 tablespoons rendered goose fat

2 cups dry white wine

1 cup water

3 pounds fresh sauerkraut

2 cloves garlic, minced

10 juniper berries, tied in a cheesecloth bag

Salt and freshly ground black pepper to taste

1 pound slab bacon in 1 piece

2 pig's knuckles, cracked (optional)

1 goose, 8 to 10 pounds

¼ cup each finely diced carrots, leek or onion, and celery

6 to 8 frankfurters

In a large pot, lightly sauté the onion in the fat. Add the wine and the water. Wash the sauerkraut very thoroughly in hot water and add to the pot with the garlic, juniper berries in cheesecloth, salt, pepper, and bacon. Cover and cook slowly for 2 hours. Remove the cheesecloth bag.

Meanwhile, if the pig's knuckles are used, cook them in boiling water until tender. Preheat the oven to 400°F and roast the goose as directed on page 182. About 20 minutes before the goose is done, add the finely chopped vegetables to pan; complete the roasting. Heat the frankfurters through. When all is ready, put the sauerkraut on a large platter. Arrange knuckles, sliced bacon, sliced goose, and frankfurters on the sauerkraut. Degrease the juices in the roasting pan, add a little broth or water, and heat. Season to taste. Pour, with the diced vegetables, over the meats. Serve with boiled potatoes.

Serves six to eight.

BLANQUETTE OF GOOSE

1 goose, 8 pounds, cut into serving pieces
1 onion, stuck with 3 cloves
1 teaspoon dried thyme
1 sprig parsley
1 lemon slice
Salt and freshly ground black pepper
Boiling water to cover
1 cup cream, blended with 2 egg yolks

🐦 Place the goose pieces in a kettle with the onion stuck with the cloves, the thyme, parsley, lemon slice, and salt and pepper to taste. Cover with boiling water, and simmer until tender, about 2 hours. Remove the goose to a hot platter or serving dish. Skim the fat off the broth and strain. Place 2 cups broth in a saucepan and bring to a boil. Simmer for 5 minutes, taste for seasoning, and add the cream mixed with the egg yolks. Stir constantly until thickened (do not allow to boil) and pour over the goose. Serve with wild rice and buttered turnips.

Serves eight.

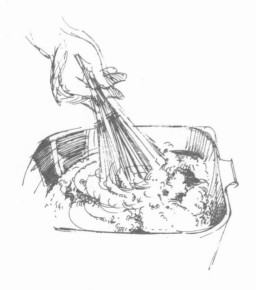

POACHED GOOSE

1 goose, 8 to 10 pounds
Savory stuffing of your choice (see pages 227–236)
Boiling water to cover
1 medium onion, finely chopped
Goose liver, chopped
¼ cup rendered goose fat or bacon fat
Salt and freshly ground black pepper
1 cup sliced mushrooms
2 tablespoons chopped parsley
1 teaspoon dried tarragon
1 cup dry white wine
Beurre manié (1 tablespoon butter kneaded with 1 tablespoon flour)

Stuff the goose with a savory stuffing of your choice. Truss (see page 125), wrap securely in a heavily floured cloth, and tie. Place in a deep pot and cover with boiling water. Simmer for 1½ to 2 hours or more, until the goose is tender.

Sauté the onion and goose liver in the goose fat or bacon fat. Season with salt and pepper to taste and add the mushrooms, parsley, tarragon, and white wine, and let simmer for 5 minutes. Add 1 cup of the degreased goose broth. Stir in the beurre manié till slightly thickened. Correct the seasoning.

Remove the goose from the kettle and unwrap. Serve on a large platter with the sauce, home-fried potatoes, and creamed turnips.

Serves eight.

NEW YEAR'S EVE GOOSE IN ASPIC

1 goose, 8 to 10 pounds

½ lemon

1 onion, stuck with 3 cloves

Bouquet garni (sprigs of parsley, thyme, tarragon, bay leaf, and garlic,
   tied in cheesecloth)

1 cup wine vinegar

Salt and freshly ground pepper

2 tablespoons (2 envelopes) unflavored gelatin, dissolved in ¼ cup cold
   water

½ cup dry white wine

Rub the goose well with half a lemon. Place the bird in a deep pot with the onion stuck with the cloves, the bouquet garni, and the wine vinegar. Cover with boiling water, and simmer till the goose is tender, 1½ to 2 hours. Add salt and pepper to taste.

Remove the goose from the pot, allow it to cool, and skin it. (The skin can be deep-fried, and the cracklings eaten as an hors d'oeuvre.) Cut the bird into serving-sized pieces and remove the meat from the bones. Arrange in a large mold. Remove all the fat from the broth, reduce it by one-half, and strain. Mix the dissolved gelatin with the white wine, and add to the broth. Taste for seasoning and pour over the goose sections in the mold. Chill. Unmold on a large platter and serve with mayonnaise and potato salad.

Serves eight.

GOOSE-POTATO SKILLET

4 tablespoons rendered goose fat

1 medium onion, finely chopped

1 green pepper, seeded and finely chopped

1½ to 2 cups finely diced roast goose

1½ pounds potatoes, boiled, peeled, and diced

Salt and freshly ground black pepper to taste

1 package (10 ounces) frozen chopped spinach, cooked and well drained

4 eggs

¼ cup milk

Heat the fat in a 10- to 12-inch skillet and sauté the onion and pepper gently until tender. Add the goose meat and potatoes and blend well. Add salt and pepper. Cover and cook over medium heat, stirring several times, for about 15 minutes, or until lightly browned. Loosely stir in the cooked spinach. Beat the eggs and the milk together and pour over the ingredients in the skillet. Cover and cook over low heat until firm. Serve cut into wedges.

Serves four.

GOOSE HASH

Leftover meat, carcass, and gravy from a roast goose

2 cups water

2 medium onions, coarsely cut

3 tablespoons rendered goose fat or butter

Any leftover stuffing

Salt and freshly ground black pepper

Cut the remnants of cold roast goose meat in small dice, and set aside. Put the carcass and leftover gravy in a pot, add the water, and simmer for 20 minutes.

Sauté the onions in the fat, then add any leftover stuffing, the goose meat, and salt and pepper to taste. Pour over this 1 cup of the cooking broth and let simmer, mixing frequently. Let cook down till rather dry. Serve with fried potatoes, cole slaw, and pickled beets or a beet and egg salad.

GOOSE TERRINE WITH FILBERTS

½ pound pork liver
½ pound boneless pork shoulder
Breast from an uncooked goose, about ½ pound after removing skin and
    bones
½ pound slab bacon
2 eggs
2 tablespoons flour
1 cup dry white wine
½ cup chopped shallots or sweet onion
½ cup whole filberts, roasted and peeled
Salt and freshly ground black pepper to taste
¼ pound or more sliced bacon
½ cup aspic (see page 192)

❧ Using the metal blade in a food processor, coarsely chop the pork liver, pork shoulder, goose, and slab bacon; or use a meat grinder. Mix thoroughly with the eggs, flour, wine, shallots, filberts, and salt and pepper.

Line a terrine or ovenproof glass casserole with the bacon slices. Press in the ground mixture. Cover and refrigerate overnight. Next day, cover with a lid or foil, set in a pan of hot water, and bake in a preheated 350°F oven for 2 hours. Uncover and drain off any excess fat. Pour ½ cup aspic over the top. Cool slightly, then refrigerate, covered, for 24 hours. Unmold on a serving plate and garnish as desired. Cut in slices to serve.

Serves eight.

Aspic

1 tablespoon (1 envelope) unflavored gelatin

2 tablespoons cold water

1 can (10¾ ounces) condensed beef bouillon

2 tablespoons Madeira or sherry

Soften the gelatin in the water. Heat all the ingredients together, stirring until the gelatin is dissolved.

Makes about 1½ cups.

GOOSE RILLETTES

1 goose, 8 to 9 pounds, roasted and cooled, reserving some rendered fat

Salt

2 to 2½ pounds pork kidney fat or leaf lard

½ cup water

1 clove garlic

Freshly ground black pepper

Dried thyme to taste (optional)

Skin the goose, and cut the meat off the bones. Sprinkle the meat with salt and let stand for several hours. Combine with the pork fat or lard, the water, garlic, pepper, and thyme (if you are using it) in a heavy casserole or braising pan. Add some of the rendered goose fat. Cook in a 300°F oven for 4 hours or until the meat has cooked down thoroughly.

Pour into a colander set over a large pan to let the meat drain. When cool, shred the meat finely, using two forks. Pack in a crock, adding some of the fat as you go. Ladle fat over the top to completely seal. This will keep for several weeks under refrigeration. Serve like a pâté on bread or toast.

LIVER-GOOSE MOLD

2 tablespoons rendered goose fat
1 pound goose and chicken livers
Salt and freshly ground black pepper to taste
1 tablespoon (1 envelope) unflavored gelatin
1¼ cups goose broth (see page 183)
1 cup finely diced roast goose
1 medium onion, chopped
½ cup cream
½ cup mayonnaise (pages 240–241)
¼ teaspoon Worcestershire sauce

Heat the fat in a skillet, add the livers, and sauté until lightly browned, seasoning with salt and pepper to taste. Set aside. Sprinkle the gelatin over ¼ cup of the cold broth. Heat the remaining 1 cup broth and mix with the softened gelatin. In a food processor, smoothly blend the gelatin mixture, goose, onion, livers, cream, and mayonnaise. (Or put the solid ingredients through a grinder, add the gelatin, cream, and mayonnaise, and blend until smooth.) Add the Worcestershire sauce and salt to taste.

Pour into a lightly oiled 1-quart mold and chill until firm. Unmold on a serving plate and garnish as desired. Serve with crisp breads or crackers. This may also be served with greens as a main dish.

LIVER PÂTÉ WITH MUSHROOMS AND HAM

3 tablespoons rendered goose fat

1 cup sliced mushrooms

½ pound chicken livers

1 large goose liver, quartered

¼ cup chopped onion

½ teaspoon salt

1 pound minced ham

Optional garnishes: Chopped hard-boiled egg, chopped pistachios, finely
sliced green onion

❧ Heat the goose fat in a large skillet and sauté the mushrooms
for 2 or 3 minutes. Add the chicken and goose livers, onion, and
salt. Cover and simmer for 6 to 8 minutes, or just until the liver
loses its pink color. Purée in a food processor or put through a meat
grinder. Stir in the ham. Spread the mixture in an oiled 3-cup terrine or mold. Cover and refrigerate several hours or overnight.
Unmold, top, if desired, with chopped hard-boiled egg, chopped pis-
tachio nuts, or finely sliced green onion, and serve with cocktail rye
bread or crackers.

GOOSE GIBLETS AND BARLEY SOUP

2 tablespoons rendered goose fat

1 cup sliced onion

Goose giblets and neck

4 cups water

1 teaspoon salt

½ teaspoon celery salt

Any leftover roast goose

1 can (1 pound) tomatoes, cut up

1 cup pearl barley

½ teaspoon dried thyme

Heat the fat in a large, heavy pot and sauté the onion until limp but not brown. Add the giblets and neck, water, salt, and celery salt. Bring to a boil, then reduce the heat, cover, and simmer for 1 hour.

Remove the neck and giblets. Cut the meat off the neck and chop the giblets fine. Return to the kettle. If desired, add leftover cut-up roast goose. Add the tomatoes, barley, and thyme. Return to a boil, reduce heat, cover, and simmer 1 additional hour.

Serves six.

CREAM OF GOOSE SOUP

2 leeks, cleaned and sliced
1 stalk celery, diced
4 tablespoons butter
2 tablespoons flour
2 quarts veal or chicken broth, or water
Carcass of 1 roast goose, plus neck and giblets
2 cups heavy cream, blended with 3 egg yolks
Salt and freshly ground black pepper

Sauté the leeks and celery in the butter in a large, heavy pot until golden. Stir in the flour and brown lightly. Add the broth, goose carcass, neck, and giblets. Bring to a boil, then reduce heat, cover, and simmer about 2 hours. Strain and put the broth back in the pot. Add the cream mixed with the egg yolks. Heat, stirring constantly, until the soup is slightly thickened; do not allow to boil. Add salt and pepper to taste.

Serves six.

Wild Goose

Wild goose may be cooked in any way that you cook domestic goose. It is often very tough, however, and requires longer cooking.

✢ CHAPTER 6 ✢
Pheasant

❦

Pheasant has a tendency to be dry and requires ample lubrication in cooking. Some sportsmen feel that it is not worth the shooting. But epicures generally favor the pheasant above most other game birds.

The battle over how long pheasant should be hung has waged on three continents for centuries. A smattering of English epicures still vow it is not fit to eat until decomposition has set in and a fetid odor is given off. I have seen pheasants in the markets of Europe so decomposed the bones had broken through and the flesh had discolored. Such birds, when cooked, have a distinct flavor that may best be described as "gamy." I prefer a pheasant that has hung about a week or 10 days, and I feel that a freshly killed bird has no distinguishing flavor.

Pheasants have been raised for shooting in England for generations. Great preserves dominated by a gamekeeper are filled with young pheasants every year and opened at the height of the season for the pleasure of the landowner and his guests. The pheasant was introduced into Europe centuries ago, in all probability from Asia, for the pheasant was originally named the Phasian bird, Phasis being a river in the ancient Asiatic province of Colchis.

In this country, pheasants are found wild in the upland states, sometimes in great profusion. Semiwild pheasants are raised in many parts of the country to supply restaurants and markets that specialize in game.

Definitely a luxury item, pheasant is worth having for any festive occasion.

Young pheasants are known by their short, rounded claws; old ones by their long and sharp ones.

Singe, draw, and clean pheasant as you do other game birds. Stuff with a savory stuffing or with celery, parsley, and onion, or just place a square of butter in each bird. One pheasant, generally 2½ to 3 pounds in weight, will serve two or three people.

ROAST PHEASANT

Singe, clean, and stuff (if desired; see pages 227–236) a young pheasant. Bard it well with salt pork or bacon, being certain that the breast, which may be dry otherwise, is well covered. Place in a roasting pan with a small piece of butter and roast for 45 to 60 minutes in a 350°F oven. Baste every 10 minutes with drippings from the pan. When the bird is tender, remove to a hot platter.

Make a sauce in the roasting pan: Skim the excess fat from the pan and add 1 cup of broth made from simmering the chopped giblets in 1½ cups salted water for 20 minutes. Blend well with the pan juices and add the chopped giblets and salt and pepper to taste. Thicken, if desired, with a beurre manié, made of 1 tablespoon butter blended with 1 tablespoon flour, and added in bits. Stir till thickened. Serve with sautéed hominy squares. Or serve with the traditional English bread sauce that follows.

Serves two or three.

BREAD SAUCE

1 small onion, cut in small pieces
2 cups milk
White bread crumbs, preferably dry
1 tablespoon butter
Salt and freshly ground black pepper
2 tablespoons heavy cream

Simmer the onion pieces gently in the milk. When the milk seems sufficiently flavored, strain to remove the onion and add enough white bread crumbs to form a sauce the consistency of heavy cream. Add the butter as the mixture cooks—the cooking will thicken it—and salt and pepper to taste. Finally stir in the heavy cream.

Makes about 2½ cups.

PHEASANT IN MADEIRA

For this dish use a heavy metal pot deep enough to enclose the bird under a tight cover.

1 young pheasant
1 large onion
1 stalk celery
Salt and freshly ground black pepper to taste
6 tablespoons butter
¼ cup chicken stock
⅓ cup Madeira

Singe and clean the pheasant, then stuff with the onion and celery and sprinkle with salt and pepper. Melt the butter in a deep braising pan and brown the pheasant evenly. Regulate the heat so that the butter browns but does not blacken. When the bird is evenly browned—about 15 minutes—turn it breast side down, clap the cover on tightly, and lower the heat. Cook, basting occasionally and turning. The bird should be done in 50 to 70 minutes in all, according to the size.

When done, remove to a hot platter and bring the pan juices to boiling. Add the stock and taste for seasoning. Then add the Madeira and bring just to boiling. Pass the sauce separately, along with a bowl of crisp buttered bread crumbs.

Serves two.

PHEASANT CASSEROLE

1 young pheasant, cut into several pieces
Flour
Salt and freshly ground black pepper
Paprika
4 tablespoons butter
3 tablespoons oil
1 cup heavy cream
2 tablespoons finely cut fresh tarragon or 1½ teaspoons dried
¼ cup Cognac

❧ Dust the pheasant in flour seasoned with salt, pepper, and paprika. Heat the butter and oil in a skillet, and brown the pheasant pieces well on all sides. Transfer to a 2-quart casserole. Remove all but 2 tablespoons of fat from the skillet, add the cream, and heat to a simmer. Add the tarragon and Cognac, and pour over the pheasant. Cover the casserole. Bake at 325°F for 1 to 1¼ hours, or until the pheasant is tender. Serve with buttered noodles or mashed potatoes.

Serves two.

BRAISED PHEASANT WITH YOGURT

1 young pheasant
3 or 4 slices of bacon
Salt and freshly ground black pepper
2 cups yogurt
3 teaspoons paprika
2 tablespoons chopped parsley

Preheat the oven to 450°F.

Singe, clean and stuff (if desired; see pages 227–236) the pheasant. Bard it well with bacon, making certain the breast is covered. Brown it in a heavy ovenproof casserole in the preheated oven for 20 minutes. Season with salt and pepper to taste and add the yogurt, paprika, and chopped parsley. Cover, reduce the heat to 325°F and cook for 25 minutes, or until tender. Serve with buttered noodles.

Serves two.

BRAISED PHEASANT WITH SAUERKRAUT

2 pounds sauerkraut, drained
2 cups chicken broth
1 cup white wine
Juniper berries
½ teaspoon caraway seeds
1 young pheasant
4 tablespoons butter
Salt and freshly ground black pepper

Preheat the oven to 350°F.

Place sauerkraut in a deep earthenware or enameled iron casserole. Add the broth, white wine, a few juniper berries, and the caraway seeds. Cover and simmer for 1 hour in the oven.

Singe and clean the pheasant. Melt the butter in a skillet and brown the bird evenly on all sides. Season with salt and pepper to taste and place in the casserole with the sauerkraut. Cover and bake until the pheasant is tender, about 45 minutes to 1 hour. Serve on a hot platter surrounded with the sauerkraut.

Serves two.

SAUTÉED PHEASANT WITH CABBAGE

1 young pheasant
6 tablespoons bacon fat or butter
1 medium head cabbage, finely shredded
Salt and freshly ground black pepper
Juniper berries (optional)
1 cup heavy cream
¼ teaspoon paprika

Singe, clean, and cut the pheasant in convenient serving pieces. Brown the pheasant in the bacon fat or butter in a large skillet. Reduce the heat, cover, and cook for 20 minutes.

Meanwhile, parboil the shredded cabbage in salted water for 10 minutes. Drain and season with salt to taste. Add the cabbage and a few juniper berries to the pheasant, cover the skillet, and allow it to cook for 10 minutes more. Add salt and pepper to taste and the cream, and simmer 5 minutes longer. Sprinkle with paprika and serve with boiled potatoes.

Serves two.

SAUTÉED PHEASANT WITH CREAM GRAVY, WESTERN STYLE

This is a typical western dish that I have enjoyed for many years and found to be one of the most delicious ways of eating pheasant. It has come down from the days when wild birds were one of the mainstays of families and were treated as everyday food rather than delicacies to be cherished and dressed up for company.

> 1 young pheasant
> Flour
> Salt and freshly ground black pepper
> 8 slices of bacon
> 2 cups rich milk or half-and-half

Singe and clean the pheasant, then cut into convenient serving pieces. Dredge with flour, salt, and pepper. Fry the bacon in a heavy skillet till crisp. Remove the bacon slices to a hot plate, and quickly brown the pieces of pheasant on both sides in the hot fat. Season with salt and pepper to taste and reduce the heat. Cover the skillet and allow the pheasant to cook slowly for 20 minutes, turning once. Remove to a hot platter and dress with the crisp bacon. Skim off all but 3 tablespoons fat from the pan juices, add 3 tablespoons flour, and blend well over medium heat. Slowly add the milk, stirring constantly, and continue to stir till the mixture thickens. Season with salt and pepper to taste and serve in a gravy boat. Mashed potatoes and buttered cabbage are good with this dish. Add hot biscuits and honey and you have a delicious pioneer meal.

Serves two.

BROILED YOUNG PHEASANT

Tender young pheasant may be split and broiled. The cooking time should be from 15 to 18 minutes. It is essential to butter the breasts well and baste frequently while broiling; otherwise you get a dry bird. Season with salt and freshly ground black pepper to taste and serve with fried hominy squares.

CHAPTER 7

Quail

୭ළ

*T*here are many varieties of quail abounding in the United States and in Europe, where they have been more popular than they ever were here. We have the bobwhite, which is prevalent in the eastern states; the crested or California quail; the valley quail; and the mountain quail. Some varieties are also called partridge. In parts of the country, domestic fresh quail are increasingly available, and I have become quite fond of serving these lovely morsels for a main course or as finger food for a cocktail party.

The English used to maintain that quail should not be drawn, and occasionally one finds an isolated case or two of the "eat the innards" school. To my knowledge, the only birds served with what is most descriptively and savagely called "the trail" are woodcock and snipe. I'll just take my birds empty or stuffed with something of my own making.

Quail should be quite fresh when cooked. The breasts need a covering of salt pork or bacon; for, like pheasant, the meat has a tendency to be dry. The roasting instructions I have given—I prefer a high temperature for small birds—should provide breast meat that is still moist and just slightly pink.

Gauge two quail per portion, unless very large, for a main course; and one, for a first course.

WHOLE ROAST QUAIL

Singe and clean quail. Place a large lump of butter and a sprig of parsley in each one and wrap the breasts well with bacon. Place on a rack in a shallow pan and roast in a preheated 475°F oven, basting frequently in the bacon fat, for 20 minutes. Remove the bacon, and return the quail to the oven for another 3 to 4 minutes. Season with salt and pepper to taste. Add to the pan juices 1 cup broth, the poached and puréed livers of the birds, and salt and pepper to taste. Heat thoroughly. Serve the quail on buttered toast, and pass the sauce separately.

Variations

1. Stuff the birds with freshly opened oysters. Proceed as above and add a little of the oyster liquor to the sauce. Serve on toast with fried parsley.
2. Bard well, place a mushroom in each bird, wrap in cooking parchment and roast for 20 minutes in a 450°F oven. Serve with sautéed mushrooms in cream.
3. Serve cold with a rémoulade sauce (see page 217) or homemade mayonnaise (see pages 240–241).

CICELY LUCAS'S QUAIL ON SCRAPPLE

A recipe that is as thoroughly American as the Bucks County farm-house from which it came.

6 quail
1 medium onion, chopped
Salt and freshly ground black pepper to taste
6 small onions
1 stalk celery, with leaves, cut in 6 pieces
6 strips bacon
1 cup good rich chicken stock
6 slices scrapple, sautéed

Preheat the oven to very hot (450°–500°F).

Singe and clean the birds, then rub with the chopped onion and salt and pepper. Stuff each bird with 1 small onion and a piece of celery with a bit of leaf as well. Lay a strip of bacon over each breast. Roast in the very hot oven, breast side up, for 5 minutes. Remove the bacon to absorbent paper. Turn the birds, breast down, add the chicken stock, and roast another 10 minutes, basting frequently. Finally turn the birds breast up once more and run under the broiler to brown, basting constantly. Do not overcook.

Remove the quail to a hot platter, arranging each bird on a slice of cooked scrapple. Garnish with the bacon. Bring the pan juices to a boil, taste for seasoning, and serve in a sauceboat.

Serves three.

SPLIT ROAST QUAIL WITH MUSTARD I

6 quail, split down the back, well cleaned (reserve the giblets), and
    flattened
Dijon mustard
12 slices bacon
Salt and freshly ground black pepper
3 tablespoons butter
Touch of Cognac
6 slices of buttered toast

🐟 Preheat the oven to 475°F.

Brush the quail breasts and legs of the quail with a fairly heavy coat of Dijon mustard, then tuck a slice of bacon over each half, covering legs, thighs, and breast section. Arrange the quail on the rack of the broiler pan, sprinkle lightly with salt and pepper, and roast in the preheated oven for 20 minutes; do not overcook. They need no basting because the bacon lubricates them. While the quail are roasting, sauté the giblets in butter until just cooked, seasoning them with salt, pepper, and a touch of Cognac, and chop them very fine.

Spread the buttered toast with a thin film of Dijon mustard and then with the sautéed, chopped giblets. Serve each quail on a piece of toast the minute they come from the oven and pour the juices left from sautéing over them.

Serve accompanied by a purée of carrots or turnip or some little Brussels sprouts, and drink a good dry white wine.

Serves three.

SPLIT ROAST QUAIL WITH MUSTARD II

8 to 10 quail, singed and cleaned
2 tablespoons Dijon mustard
2 tablespoons olive oil
16 to 20 slices bacon
Salt and freshly ground black pepper to taste

🍂 Preheat the oven to 475°F.

Split the quail and remove the wing tips. Brush with a blend of Dijon mustard and olive oil. Lay a strip of bacon around each half. Place on a rack in a small pan, skin side up, and roast in the preheated oven 20 minutes. Season with salt and pepper to taste. Serve as an entrée or as a cocktail hors d'oeuvre to be eaten with the fingers and with the aid of plenty of paper napkins.

Serves four to five as an entrée.

BROILED QUAIL

Singe, clean, and draw each quail, split down the back, and flatten. Rub well with butter or oil and place a goodly amount in the hollow of the rib cage. Broil for 8 to 10 minutes, turning several times and basting with butter. Season with salt and pepper to taste. Serve with braised celery.

SAUTÉED QUAIL WITH MADEIRA

2 quail
4 tablespoons butter
Salt and freshly ground black pepper
¼ cup Madeira
2 tablespoons finely cut orange zest
2 slices buttered toast

🍂 Singe, clean, and split the quail down the back as for broiling. Melt the butter in a skillet and brown the quail very quickly on both sides over brisk heat. Reduce the heat and sauté gently for about 10 minutes. Season with salt and pepper to taste and add the Madeira and orange zest. Turn the quail well in this mixture. Serve on toast.

Serves one.

SAUTÉED QUAIL WITH JUNIPER BERRIES

7 tablespoons butter

6 quail, cleaned, livers reserved

Salt and freshly ground black pepper

1 to 2 tablespoons chopped juniper berries

1 to 1½ cups water or broth, as needed

6 slices buttered toast

Melt 6 tablespoons butter in a large skillet and brown the quail very quickly, turning the birds from side to side so they attain an evenness of color. Season with salt and pepper to taste and add the juniper berries. Cover, reduce the heat, and let them cook for 10 minutes.

Meanwhile, poach the quail livers till tender in salted water or broth to barely cover. Purée, add a tablespoon of butter, and keep warm. Serve the quail on buttered toast lightly spread with the liver purée, and pass the pan juices separately.

Serves three.

SAUTÉ OF QUAIL WITH WHITE GRAPES

6 slices stale bread about 2 inches thick

6 quail, singed and cleaned

6 tablespoons butter

Salt and freshly ground black pepper

½ cup chicken broth

6 tablespoons Cognac

1 cup seedless white grapes

❧ Make oval croustades of dry bread. They should be about 2 inches thick and just a bit larger than the quail. Hollow out a shallow cavity into which the quail will fit and toast the croustades gently in a slow oven. Butter the cavity into which you place the bird.

Brown the birds very quickly in butter. Season with salt and pepper to taste and add the broth. Cover, reduce the heat, and simmer for 10 minutes. Pour the Cognac over the birds and blaze them. Add the white grapes and shake the pan to coat them with the juices. Serve the quail and grapes in the croustades, and pass the pan juices separately.

Serves three.

BREAST OF QUAIL SAUTÉ

Breast meat of 12 quail

8 tablespoons butter

3 tablespoons chopped shallots

Salt and freshly ground black pepper

8 slices toast

❧ Sauté the quail breasts in the butter for 5 to 6 minutes. Add the shallots and salt and pepper to taste. Cook briskly for another 2 minutes. Serve on toast.

Serves four.

BRAISED STUFFED QUAIL WITH WHITE WINE

8 quail
2 teaspoons chopped shallots
8 tablespoons butter
8 mushrooms, finely chopped
1 tablespoon chopped parsley
1 cup dry bread crumbs
Salt and freshly ground black pepper
Fresh tarragon
Pinch of freshly grated nutmeg
½ cup blanched, sliced almonds
1⅓ cups white wine
8 croustades or slices of toast

Preheat the oven to 375°F.

Singe and clean the quail. Make a stuffing by sautéing the chopped shallots in 2 tablespoons butter. Add the mushrooms, chopped parsley, and bread crumbs, salt and pepper to taste, a few leaves of fresh tarragon, nutmeg, almonds, and ⅓ cup white wine.

Stuff the quail. Melt 6 tablespoons butter in an ovenproof skillet and brown the birds very quickly. Turn them breast side down and add 1 cup of white wine. Roast in the preheated oven for 15 minutes. Turn the birds breast side up and increase the heat to 450°F for 3 to 4 minutes. Season with salt and pepper to taste and serve in croustades or on toast. Serve the pan juices separately.

Serves four

✦ CHAPTER 8 ✦
Partridge

Many gallinaceous birds in this country are called partridge through ignorance or custom or for want of a better name. Hence, the bobwhite quail is called partridge in some locales. The bone structure and quality of flesh is similar in the two game birds, but there is a difference in plumage and coloring.

Wild partridge eaten before it has hung for 3 to 5 days is a rather dull and uninteresting dish. It needs the gamy quality to bring out the flavor. However, domestically raised partridge can be obtained fresh from game farms during most of the year—it will improve in flavor if hung for 5 or 6 days—and it is also sold frozen.

One partridge makes an adequate serving. Wild rice, mushrooms, cabbage, and carrots are all good accompaniments. In all honesty, I have seldom eaten tender partridge. It tends to be tough, and especially with wild partridge, one must look for young birds.

ROAST PARTRIDGE

Singe and clean partridges. Rub well, inside and out, with lemon juice or half a lemon, and put a lump of butter in each cavity. Wrap salt pork or bacon around the breasts and secure with string. Push the legs toward the breasts, and secure them with a skewer pushed through the middle of the birds. Place on their sides on a rack in a roasting pan, and roast at 450°F for 10 minutes, basting with butter. Turn to other side and roast for 10 minutes, again basting. Then remove the salt pork or bacon and turn breast side up for a final 10 minutes. Serve with bread sauce (page 198) or with the degreased pan juices mixed with the poached chopped giblets and salt and freshly ground black pepper to taste. Allow 1 bird per person.

Variations

1. Serve with cabbage, prepared in this fashion: Place 1 shredded head of cabbage, 4 scraped, diced carrots, and a medium onion stuck with cloves in a kettle with ½ pound pork, 6 bacon slices cut in strips, and 1 cup chicken broth. Cover and simmer for 1½ hours. Add ½ cup white wine after the first hour of cooking. Season with salt and freshly ground black pepper to taste. Arrange the roasted partridges on the cooked cabbage on a large hot platter. Serve with the degreased pan juices mixed with the poached, chopped giblets.
2. Serve with grilled, well-seasoned sausages and watercress.
3. Serve with grilled mushroom caps.

BROILED PARTRIDGE

Singe and clean young partridges, allowing 1 bird per portion. Split down the back and flatten. Rub well with butter. Place on a broiling rack in a preheated broiler and broil, skin side down, for 8 minutes. Season with salt and freshly ground black pepper to taste, then turn, baste with butter, and broil for another 7 or 8 minutes, till nicely browned and tender.

Meanwhile, poach the giblets till tender with an onion stuck with 2 cloves in 2 cups water. Chop the giblets fine and mix with 1 tablespoon butter and a little of the broth in which you cooked them. Spread slices of crisp well-buttered toast with this mixture and place half a partridge on a slice of toast. Pour over it the drippings from the pan and serve.

BROILED DEVILED PARTRIDGE

Singe and clean young partridges, then split down the back and flatten. Rub well with butter and place, skin side down, on a rack in a preheated broiler. Broil for 8 minutes. Turn, baste with butter, and broil for 5 minutes, or until nearly done. Remove and season with salt and pepper to taste. Brush well with butter and then coat with toasted crumbs. Replace in the broiler for 2 or 3 minutes to brown slightly. Serve with deviled sauce (see page 216).

Deviled Sauce

½ cup white wine
2 tablespoons wine vinegar
1 bay leaf
6 peppercorns
1 small onion, stuck with 2 cloves
2 tablespoons flour
2 tablespoons butter
1 cup chicken broth
Salt and cayenne pepper to taste

Boil together the white wine, vinegar, bay leaf, peppercorns, and onion stuck with the cloves. When reduced to half, remove from the heat and strain. Blend the flour with the butter in a saucepan over medium heat, and let brown. Add the broth and stir well until thickened. Add the strained flavoring and blend well. Season with salt to taste and generous sprinkling of cayenne.

COLD PARTRIDGE WITH RÉMOULADE SAUCE

4 partridges
1 onion, finely chopped
2 tablespoons butter
Giblets, poached in salted water and chopped
2 tablespoons chopped parsley
Juniper berries, crushed
1 cup fresh bread crumbs
¼ cup pine nuts
¼ cup sherry

🐦 Preheat the oven to 450°F.

Singe and clean the birds. Make a stuffing by sautéing the onion in the butter; then adding the poached, chopped giblets, parsley, a few crushed juniper berries, and the fresh bread crumbs. Mix well, remove from the heat, and add the pine nuts and sherry. Stuff the birds and secure them. Roast according to the recipe on page 214; cool, but do not refrigerate.

Serve with rémoulade sauce or Cumberland sauce (see page 218) and green salad. This is an excellent supper or picnic dish.

Serves four.

Rémoulade Sauce

1½ cups mayonnaise
1 tablespoon finely chopped parsley
2 tablespoons finely chopped capers
1 hard-boiled egg, finely chopped
Lemon juice to taste
Salt and freshly ground black pepper to taste

🐦 Blend all the ingredients well. For a more piquant flavor, omit the salt and add 2 or 3 finely chopped anchovies.

Makes about 2 cups.

Cumberland Sauce

Zest and juice of 1 orange
1 cup Madeira or port
1 tablespoon lemon juice
½ cup currant jelly
Pinch of cayenne or ground ginger

Cut the zest off the orange and chop it finely. Cook with the Madeira or port until the wine is reduced by one-third. Add the orange juice, lemon juice, currant jelly, and a small pinch of cayenne or ground ginger. Heat until the jelly is melted, and blend well. Serve cold.

Makes about 2 cups.

CHAPTER 9

Snipe and Woodcock

❦

Snipe are found in the coastal regions of the United States, but are comparatively little known in other parts of the country, hence they have never been as popular here as in England and France, where they are treasured. They are particularly popular with sportsmen for they are excellent shooting; their fast and irregular flight makes them a game bird almost without equal.

The snipe, which weighs from 2½ ounces to 8 ounces, has a long and functional beak which it uses for digging worms and bugs in bogs, swamps, and marshlands. The breast, truly the only worthwhile portion of the bird, is full and well-flavored. One snipe is a portion, though there are those who will eat more than that at a sitting.

Snipe are generally hung for 3 or 4 days. Like woodcock, they are seldom drawn. Those who are fond of eating them feel that the intestines and the giblets, called "the trail," give added flavor. They are sometimes drawn after they are cooked and the intestines chopped and mixed with the sauce in the pan. Traditionally they are cooked with the beak skewering the middle of the bird. The English favor bread sauce (page 198) or a dish of hot buttered crumbs served with the birds.

BROILED SNIPE

Singe and clean the birds. Do not draw, but remove the gizzard. Rub well with butter and broil in a preheated broiler for 12 to 15 minutes. Baste well with butter or fat during broiling, and turn often so an evenness of color is assured on all sides. Serve on fried toast with bread sauce (page 198) or with a tart jelly and hominy squares, if you prefer. They are also delicious served on a crisp slice of scrapple.

ROAST SNIPE I

Singe and clean the birds. Do not draw, but remove the gizzard. Cover the breasts with salt pork or bacon and place in a buttered baking dish. Place in a 475°F oven and roast for 20 minutes. Season with salt and pepper to taste. Serve with the pan juices.

Variations

1. When the snipe are cooked, remove the intestines and cut them into fine pieces. Sauté them in the fat from the baking dish and season to taste. Add ¼ cup Cognac and mix well. Pour the sauce over the birds on a heated platter and add another ¼ cup Cognac. Flambé and serve.
2. Follow the first variation, but add 1 tablespoon minced shallots to the sauce. Cut the birds in half and bathe them well in the sauce. Flambé.
3. Add ½ cup Madeira to the pan juices. Heat and serve.
4. Baste the snipe with a little orange juice during cooking and add finely cut shreds of orange zest and ½ cup Madeira to the sauce.

ROAST SNIPE II

Singe, draw and clean the snipe. Put 2 or 3 juniper berries in the cavity, brush the skin with oil, and season with salt and pepper. Roast on a rack for 20 minutes in a 475°F oven, basting two or three times with oil or butter. Remove from the oven, and flame with gin. Serve on fried toast.

SALMI OF SNIPE

Snipe, singed and cleaned, giblets reserved if desired
6 to 7 tablespoons butter
2 tablespoons finely chopped shallots
1 clove garlic, finely chopped
1 cup chicken broth
Salt and freshly ground black pepper
3 tablespoons flour
½ cup Madeira or sherry
Juniper berries
Pinch of ground cloves
Pinch of ground ginger

Roast or broil snipe as directed on pages 220–221, then season and serve with the following sauce: Heat 3 tablespoons butter in a skillet. Add the shallots and garlic and sauté till transparent. Add the broth and simmer for 5 minutes. Strain, and season with salt and pepper to taste. In a saucepan over medium heat, blend an additional 3 tablespoons butter and the flour. Gradually stir in the strained broth and Madeira or sherry, and stir till properly thickened. Add a few juniper berries and the cloves and ginger.

Let the birds cook in this sauce for 5 to 6 minutes, adding the pan juices. You may also add the chopped giblets, sautéed in 1 tablespoon of butter.

Woodcock

Woodcock is a small game bird, related to the snipe, that is much relished in England and France. Although they are not easy to come by in the United States, I have eaten them in New York and in the South. They are a nuisance to pick if you get them in feather but are well worth the trouble. After cleaning them, wrap in a damp towel, and store in the refrigerator for 4 to 5 days to mature in flavor. They can be prepared according to any of the recipes given for snipe.

ॐ

✢ CHAPTER 10 ✢
Dove

૨ⓢ

Dove has always had a great public in the South. It is a fine target for the hunter and a rewarding dish for the food fancier. Oftentimes, however, it is overcooked, to become a rather unappetizing dish—the fault of recipes inherited from the past. This delicate bird requires very little elaboration; it is best when cooked simply.

BARBECUED OR BROILED DOVES

6 doves

½ lemon

1 cup finely chopped tart apple

¾ cup finely chopped onion

1 teaspoon salt

Freshly ground black pepper

¼ teaspoon freshly grated nutmeg

¼ cup melted butter

12 slices bacon

½ cup medium-dry sherry or Madeira

Singe and clean the doves, then rub the cavities well with the half a lemon. Combine the apple, onion, seasonings, and butter, and spoon into the birds. Wrap 2 slices of bacon around each and place on a broiling rack. Grill over medium coals, or about 6 inches from the broiling unit. Turn them often till nicely colored. Transfer to a rack in a roasting pan or heated casserole. Add the sherry or Madeira, cover, and braise in a 250°F oven for 10 minutes. Pour the pan juices over the birds. Serve with corn pudding or spoon bread and a salad.

Serves six.

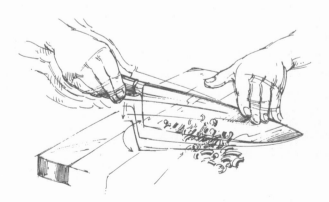

BRAISED DOVE

This is a delightful way to treat small game birds, and really no trouble.

> 2 slices bacon, cut in small pieces
> 1 shallot, very finely chopped
> 2½ tablespoons chopped parsley
> 4 small white onions
> Dried thyme
> 3 tablespoons butter
> 2 doves, cleaned and drawn
> Dried sweet basil
> Dried chervil
> ⅔ cup chicken broth
> 1 tablespoon glace de viande (concentrated beef glaze)
> ½ cup pitted green olives

Preheat the oven to 450°F.

Cook the bacon very gently in a flameproof baking dish with the chopped shallot and 1½ tablespoons chopped parsley. Add the onions and a pinch of thyme, toss to blend, and allow the onions to brown very slightly. Pour off the bacon fat and remove bacon bits to a warm dish. Heat 1 tablespoon butter in the baking dish, and sear the birds very quickly.

Mix the remaining butter with a pinch of thyme, sweet basil, chervil, and another tablespoon of parsley. Divide in half and insert in the cavity of each bird. Pour the chicken broth over them. Place in a hot 450°F oven, and bake for 12 minutes. If the broth cooks down too quickly, add more.

Finally, add the glace de viande to the pan juices, along with the bacon bits and olives. Cook up very quickly, correct the seasoning, and remove the birds to a warm platter. Skim off the excess fat from the sauce, and serve with the birds.

Serves two.

CHAPTER 11

Stuffings

BASIC BREAD STUFFING

For Turkey

One of the simplest and best stuffings is prepared the following way. Gauge about ½ to ¾ cup of stuffing per pound of turkey.

2 large onions, finely chopped
10 tablespoons butter
9 cups stale bread crumbs or toasted crumbs
2½ cups finely cut celery
2½ teaspoons dried thyme and marjoram, mixed
2½ tablespoons chopped parsley
Salt and freshly ground black pepper

Sauté the onions in 2½ tablespoons butter till transparent. Add the remaining butter, allow to melt, and blend with the crumbs and seasonings.

Makes about 12 to 13 cups.

Variations

1. Add ⅓ cup chopped green pepper or pimiento.
2. Add 2½ cups sliced mushrooms, sautéed in 8 tablespoons butter.
3. Add 1¼ cups diced smoked ham, sautéed in a little fat.
4. Add 1¼ cups crisply fried bacon slivers.
5. Add 1¼ cups blanched almonds.
6. Add 1¼ cups salted peanuts.
7. Add 1¼ cups coarsely chopped tart apple.
8. Add the chopped giblets of the bird, sautéed in butter.
9. Substitute cornbread for the bread crumbs.
10. Add 2½ cups sausage meat, browned quickly in the skillet.
11. Add 1¼ cups raisins, soaked in sherry.

TARRAGON CRUMB STUFFING
For Turkey

2 cups finely chopped scallions or shallots

¾ pound butter

10 cups fresh bread crumbs, preferably from French or Italian bread,
   part whole-wheat if desired

1 tablespoon or more dried tarragon

½ cup chopped parsley

2 teaspoons salt, or to taste

1 teaspoon freshly ground black pepper

Sherry, Cognac, or turkey broth, if needed

~ Place the scallions or shallots in a skillet with the butter, and heat until the butter is melted. Blend with the crumbs, herbs, and seasonings and toss well. Taste for salt. If the stuffing is too dry, moisten with a bit of sherry, Cognac, or turkey broth.

Makes about 14 cups.

SAUSAGE STUFFING
For Turkey

2 pounds good sausage meat

1½ teaspoons salt

1 teaspoon dried thyme

1 teaspoon Tabasco

1 teaspoon ground coriander

1 teaspoon freshly ground black pepper

1 pound ground veal or ham

¾ cup pine nuts

½ cup finely chopped parsley

~ Blend all ingredients thoroughly. Test for seasoning by sautéing about 2 teaspoons in butter.

Makes about 7 or 8 cups.

BRAZIL NUT STUFFING
For Turkey
3 cups bread crumbs, toasted

1 cup ground fresh pork without fat

4 tablespoons butter

4 large white onions, finely chopped

½ cup sliced mushrooms

½ cup chopped celery

½ teaspoon dried thyme

½ teaspoon dried rosemary

Salt and freshly ground black pepper to taste

1 cup Brazil nuts

½ cup sherry, or as needed

❧ Mix the bread crumbs with the pork. Heat the butter in a large skillet and sauté the chopped onions till transparent. Add the mushrooms, celery, and herbs. Blend well over low heat. Add to the crumb and pork mixture and season well with salt and pepper. If you want to taste for salt, sauté a small amount; do not eat raw.

Blanch the Brazil nuts by immersing them in boiling water. Slip the skins off with fingers or a dull knife. Add them to the mixture, along with enough sherry to moisten thoroughly.

Makes 8 to 9 cups.

POTATO STUFFING
For Goose or Turkey
4 tart apples, cored, peeled, and quartered

4 medium onions, chopped

2 cups broth (made from the neck and giblets simmered in water)

1 sprig parsley

½ teaspoon dried thyme

½ teaspoon dried rosemary

3 cups hot riced potatoes

2 tablespoons butter

⤙ Simmer the apples and onions in the broth till tender. Add the parsley, thyme, and rosemary. Force through a fine sieve and mix with the hot riced potatoes. Add the butter and whip until fluffy.

Makes about 8 cups.

CHESTNUT STUFFING
For Goose or Turkey

1 pound unshelled chestnuts

1 large onion, finely chopped

8 tablespoons butter

2 tablespoons chopped parsley

½ teaspoon dried thyme

½ teaspoon dried rosemary

Salt and freshly ground black pepper

3 cups dry bread crumbs

Giblets, chopped and sautéed in butter (optional)

⤙ Slit the skin crosswise on the flat side of each chestnut, and roast or boil the chestnuts till tender. (Roasting them is my preference.) Shell and skin them and break into bits.

Sauté the onion in 4 tablespoons butter till transparent. Add the herbs. Blend with the dry bread crumbs and chestnuts, and salt and pepper to taste. Lubricate with the remaining butter, melted. Add chopped sautéed giblets if you like.

Makes 7 to 8 cups.

OYSTER STUFFING
For Turkey

1 large onion, finely chopped

2 tablespoons chopped green pepper

3 tablespoons butter or rendered fat from the bird

¼ pound bacon, cut in tiny slivers

3 cups dry bread crumbs

Salt and freshly ground black pepper

½ teaspoon dried thyme

1 quart raw oysters, chopped

½ cup oyster liquor

Sauté the onion and green pepper in the butter or rendered fat. In another skillet, fry out the bacon slivers until crisp. Add the bacon, onion, and green pepper to the dry bread crumbs and season to taste. Add the chopped oysters and oyster liquor and mix well.

Makes about 10 cups.

RICE GIBLET STUFFING
For Turkey

1½ cups raw rice

Giblets, very finely chopped

1 large onion, very finely chopped

1 clove garlic, very finely chopped

4 tablespoons butter

½ cup chopped parsley

½ teaspoon dried thyme

½ teaspoon dried rosemary

½ teaspoon dried marjoram

Pinch of ground ginger

Salt and freshly ground black pepper

½ cup broken walnut meats

～ Cook the rice in boiling, salted water till fluffy and tender.

Sauté the giblets, onion, and garlic in the butter until delicately browned. Add to the rice, along with the parsley, thyme, rosemary, marjoram, ginger, and salt and pepper to taste. Last, add the walnut meats and mix well.

Makes about 7 cups.

SIMPLE APPLE STUFFING
For Wild Duck
Equal quantities of chopped apple, onion, and celery mixed with a little rosemary and marjoram and lightly dusted with mace and nutmeg make a superb stuffing for duck or almost any wild game bird.

NUTTED HAM STUFFING
For Capon, Chicken or a Small Turkey
1 medium onion, finely chopped
3 tablespoons butter
½ pound smoked ham, ground
1 cup chopped celery
1½ cups fresh bread crumbs
½ cup pine nuts
½ cup sherry
½ teaspoon dried rosemary
Salt and freshly ground black pepper

～ Sauté the onion in butter. Mix with ham and the other ingredients and season to taste.

Makes about 5 cups.

MATZOH STUFFING
FOR CHICKEN OR TURKEY

Giblets, chopped

2 onions, finely chopped

3 tablespoons butter or rendered fat from the bird

Salt and freshly ground black pepper

5 to 8 matzohs or dry water biscuits

4 egg yolks, beaten

¼ teaspoon dried thyme

¼ teaspoon dried marjoram

Pinch of freshly grated nutmeg

1 tablespoon grated fresh ginger

Sauté the chopped giblets and onions in the butter or rendered fat from the bird. Season with salt and pepper to taste. Transfer the giblets and onions to a dish.

Soak matzohs or dry water biscuits in water. Drain, squeeze dry, and add to the fat in the pan in which you sautéed the giblets. Stir well over a very low flame and add to the giblets. Add the egg yolks, herbs, and spices. Blend well and correct the seasoning.

Makes about 4 cups.

APPLE AND CHESTNUT STUFFING
FOR GOOSE

Pare, core, and halve 4 to 12 apples, according to the size of your bird. Slit the skins of 1 to 2 pounds of chestnuts. Boil till tender and skin them. Sprinkle with salt and freshly grated nutmeg. Alternate the apples and chestnuts inside the bird and pack very tightly. Sew up the vent and roast. The apples and chestnuts will blend into a most delectable stuffing. A few prunes soaked in white wine for 6 hours may be added, if desired.

SWEET POTATO AND MINCEMEAT STUFFING
FOR DUCK, GOOSE, OR TURKEY

4 cups mashed and buttered sweet potatoes

1 cup coarsely chopped tart apples

2 cups mincemeat

½ cup brandy

½ teaspoon mace

½ teaspoon ground ginger

🌶 Blend the sweet potatoes with the tart apples, and mix in the mincemeat flavored with the brandy, mace, and ginger.

Makes about 7 cups.

SAUERKRAUT STUFFING
FOR DUCK OR GOOSE

In many European countries, sauerkraut has long been a traditional stuffing for duck and goose, as well as pheasant and turkey. It provides a delicious complementary flavor.

1 large onion, thinly sliced

¼ cup butter or other fat

1 pound sauerkraut

1 teaspoon caraway seeds

1 tart apple, finely chopped

1 cup white wine

🌶 Sauté the onion in the butter or other fat. When nicely browned, add the sauerkraut, caraway seeds, and apple. Toss well in the pan for 5 minutes, then add the white wine and simmer for 5 minutes more.

Makes 6 to 7 cups.

DUXELLES

2 pounds mushrooms
½ pound unsalted butter
1 large shallot, finely chopped
Salt and freshly ground black pepper

❧ Wipe the mushrooms with a damp cloth, then chop both caps and stems very fine. Put in dish towel and squeeze out the moisture. Heat the butter in a heavy skillet, and add the mushrooms and chopped shallot. Cook over low heat, stirring from time to time, until reduced to a thick, dark paste. Season with salt and pepper. Store in a jar and refrigerate—it will keep for a week—or freeze until ready to use.

Makes 3 cups.

✛ CHAPTER 12 ✛
Basic Sauces

BÉCHAMEL SAUCE (BASIC WHITE SAUCE)
2 tablespoons butter
2 tablespoons flour
1 cup milk, broth, or other liquid, heated
Salt and freshly ground black pepper
Freshly grated nutmeg

Melt the butter in a heavy saucepan over low heat and stir in the flour. Blend well for 2 or 3 minutes and gradually add the hot milk or broth. Increase the heat slightly and stir until the mixture is smooth and thickened. Allow to simmer for 3 or 4 minutes more. Season with salt and pepper to taste, and add a few grains of nutmeg.

Makes 1 cup.

Note: For a thick white sauce, use 1 tablespoon more of butter and flour.

Variations

1. *Velouté Sauce:* Add ½ cup heavy cream to the béchamel sauce, simmer for a few minutes, and then beat in 3 tablespoons butter, one at a time.
2. *Sauce Suprême:* Use rich chicken broth for the liquid in making the béchamel sauce. Combine 3 lightly beaten egg yolks with 1 cup heavy cream. Stir in a little of the sauce to warm the eggs, and then stir this mixture back into the sauce. Simmer over low heat, but do not allow to boil.
3. *Mornay Sauce:* To the béchamel sauce, add ¼ to ½ cup freshly grated Parmesan cheese and blend thoroughly.
4. *Cheese Sauce:* Add ½ cup grated sharp Cheddar or Swiss cheese to the béchamel sauce, and heat just until the cheese melts.

HOLLANDAISE SAUCE

3 or 4 egg yolks
½ teaspoon salt
1 or 2 tablespoons lemon juice
Dash of Tabasco
8 tablespoons butter, cut into small pieces
1 tablespoon hot or cold water, if needed

Hand Method

Place a small, heavy saucepan (enameled cast-iron preferred) over low heat or the top of a double boiler over hot, not boiling, water. Put 3 egg yolks, the salt, 1 tablespoon lemon juice, and Tabasco in the pan and beat with a wire whisk or electric hand mixer until well blended and the eggs have slightly thickened. Have the butter ready on a warm plate. Start adding the butter, beating in a piece at a time until it is absorbed. Do not add too quickly. Continue to beat until the sauce is thick. If it is too thick, add a tablespoon of cold water.

Blender Method

Use the ingredients given above, with 1 tablespoon lemon juice and adding the extra egg yolk. Combine all the ingredients except the butter and water in the blender container. Turn on and off at high speed just long enough to blend. Heat the butter in a saucepan until it is hot and foaming, but do not allow it to brown. Turn the blender to high speed, and very slowly and steadily pour in the butter. If the sauce curdles, add 1 tablespoon hot water while blending.

Food Processor Method

Use the ingredients given above, adding the extra egg yolk and extra tablespoon of lemon juice. Process all the ingredients except the butter and water for a few seconds, using the metal blade. Then continue to process while you gradually pour in hot, foaming (not browned) butter.

Makes about 1 cup.

SAUCE BÉARNAISE

1 tablespoon finely chopped shallots or scallions
1 tablespoon chopped fresh tarragon, more if desired, or 1 teaspoon dried
¼ cup wine vinegar
¼ cup white wine
1 teaspoon chopped parsley
Hollandaise sauce (see page 238)

Combine the shallots or scallions, tarragon, wine vinegar, white wine, and chopped parsley. Bring to a boil and reduce to practically a glaze, about 2 tablespoons. Add this to the hollandaise sauce, just before you add the butter. If tarragon is fresh, it is sometimes pleasant to stir an extra amount into the finished sauce.

Makes about 1 cup.

HOMEMADE MAYONNAISE

Hand Method

2 egg yolks

1 teaspoon salt

½ teaspoon dry mustard

1½ cups good olive oil, or a mixture of olive oil and vegetable oil

1 tablespoon lemon juice or white wine vinegar

🐦 Put the egg yolks, salt, and mustard in a bowl and beat with a wire whisk or hand beater till the yolks have thickened. Begin to add the oil a few drops at a time, beating after each addition, until the mixture begins to emulsify and thicken, at which point the oil can be added in tablespoons. After all the oil has been incorporated, beat in the lemon juice or vinegar. This will keep 1 week under refrigeration.

Note: If the emulsion separates, start over with 1 egg yolk in a clean bowl, beating in a bit of oil and then the original mixture.

Makes 1¾ cups.

Blender Method

2 eggs

1 teaspoon salt

½ teaspoon dry mustard

1 tablespoon lemon juice or white wine vinegar

1½ cups olive oil, or a mixture of olive oil and vegetable oil

🐦 Put the eggs, salt, mustard, and lemon juice or vinegar in the container of the blender, and run at high speed for about 5 seconds. Remove the cover insert, turn on the blender, and pour in the oil in a very thin, steady stream. Blend until the emulsion is smooth and then turn off at once.

Makes about 2 cups.

Food Processor Method

1 egg
1 tablespoon white wine vinegar
½ teaspoon dry mustard
½ teaspoon salt
¼ teaspoon freshly ground white pepper
1 cup olive oil

🐌 Put the egg, vinegar, mustard, salt, and pepper in the bowl of the food processor, fitted with the metal blade. Process about 2 to 3 seconds, or until blended; then, very slowly at first, pour the oil through feed tube until it has all been incorporated and the emulsion has thickened. Taste for seasoning.

Note: If the mayonnaise should separate, put 2 egg yolks in a clean bowl, start to process, and gradually pour in the original mixture.

Makes about 1¼ cups.

Editor's Note: Uncooked eggs can harbor salmonella bacteria, a possible source of food poisoning. To avoid risk, you might want to seek out a mayonnaise recipe that calls for lightly cooked yolks.

Index

with thighs, in Hungarian chicken, 66
with yogurt, 20
Leonie de Sounin's herbed broilers, 49
in lettuce leaves, 95
livers
  en brochette, 109
  chopped, 113
  in liver-goose mold, 193
  pâté, with mushrooms and ham, 194
  pâté, with pork, 112
  quick pâté, 112–113
  sauté of, 110
Maryland, 26–27
mayonnaise, 101
mushroom soup, 121
mustard chicken, baked, 84
pan-fried, 30
  Clay Triplette's, 30
panné, 35
parts, availability of, xvii
pâté(s)
  liver and pork, 112
  quick, 112–113
pie(s)
  French, 96
  old-fashioned, 98
  Pennsylvania, 97
  special, 99
poached
  chicken breasts, stuffed, 43–44
  chicken in the pot, 39–40
  Creole chicken, 46–47
  in djaj m'kalli, 44–45
  with dumplings, 36–37
  farm style, 41
  with rice, 38
  with spaghetti, 42–43
in the pot, 39–40
quality of, current, xv–xvi
quiche, 100
roast, 55–56
  with bacon, 56
  diet, 58
  giblet sauce for, 57
  with herbed butter, 56
  sesame, 59
  squab chicken, with curried rice, 60
  stuffings for, 56, 233, 234–235
roasters, notes on, 2
salad(s), 101
  chicken mayonnaise, 101
  hot, 94
  sandwich, 104
  simple, 101
  traditional, 101
sandwich(es)
  chicken salad, 104

club house sandwich, 103
composed sandwich, 104
my favorite, 103
toasted, 104
sauté(s)
  basic, 4
  with cabbage, a, 12
  with curry and tomato sauce, a, 14
  with ham, 12–13
  Jeanne Owen's, with tarragon, 6
  lemon, a, 7
  with mushrooms, a, 8
  with onions, a, 11
  with oysters, a, 13
  with peppers, a, 10
  southwestern, a, 15
  with tomato, a, 6–7
  Viennese, a, 14
  with white wine and herbs, a, 5
  see also sautéed (chicken), below
sauté(ed)
  chicken breasts Armagnac, 18
  chicken breasts with mushroom sauce,
    16–17
  chicken breasts, stuffed, 34
  chicken wings, 21
  chicken Yucatan, 19
  vs. fried, 3
  John Beard's, 22–23
  notes on, 3
  see also sautés, above
soufflé, 108
soup(s)
  chicken mushroom soup, 121
  a rich cream of, 120
  see also broth, consommé, above
Southwestern sauté, 15
squab
  deviled, with sauce béarnaise, 52
  notes on, 1
  roast, with curried rice, 60
  sautéed, 22
  stuffed, 61
stuffings for, 56, 233, 235
Swiss enchiladas, 90
teriyaki, 50
terrapin (creamed chicken with eggs), 91
Tetrazzini, 83
wings
  in paella, 74–75
  sautéed, 21
Yucatan, 19
see also Capon; Cornish game hen; Fowl
Chili, turkey, 141–142
Chocolate. See Turkey mole
Chopped giblet sandwich, 111
Cicely Lucas's quail on scrapple, 207

About the Author

Born in Portland, Oregon, in 1903, James Beard was destined to find his calling in the food profession. He acquired a sophisticated palate while still a boy, thanks to the good example of his mother, who had run a small residence hotel with a fine kitchen, but he first aspired to be a singer and then an actor. He failed to make his mark as either, and in the late 1930s joined two friends in a catering service in New York. It was called Hors D'Oeuvre, Inc. and led to the publication in 1940 of his first book, *Hors d'Oeuvre and Canapés*, which remained in print for nearly sixty years and has become a classic. More than twenty cookbooks followed, including the best-selling *James Beard Cookbook, James Beard's American Cookery, James Beard's Theory and Practice of Good Cooking* and *Beard on Bread*. In 1946 Beard appeared on television's first cooking program, and in the 1950s he started the classes that grew into his renowned cooking school. Throughout his career he was sought after as a consultant by restaurants and food producers. On behalf of the latter he toured the country continuously, giving lectures and food demonstrations. He was an exponent of simple, honest cooking, using the best ingredients, and an early believer in the existence of genuine American cuisine. By the time he died, in 1985, he was generally acknowledged to be the country's most influential food authority.